LION IN THE STREETS

Also by Judith Thompson

LION IN THE STREETS
JUDITH THOMPSON

PLAYWRIGHTS CANADA PRESS
TORONTO

For professional or amateur production rights, please contact:
Great North Artists Management
350 Dupont St.
Toronto, ON M5R 1V9
416.925.2051

LIBRARY AND ARCHIVES CANADA CATALOGUING IN PUBLICATION
Thompson, Judith, 1954-, author
    Lion in the streets / Judith Thompson. -- Second edition.

A play.
Issued in print and electronic formats.
ISBN 978-1-77091-274-8 (pbk.).--ISBN 978-1-77091-275-5 (pdf).--ISBN 978-1-77091-276-2 (epub)

    I. Title.

PS8589.H527L56 2014   C812'.54   C2014-904116-0
                                        C2014-904117-9

Playwrights Canada Press acknowledges that we operate on land which, for thousands of years, has been the traditional territories of the Mississaugas of the New Credit, the Huron-Wendat, the Anishinaabe, Métis, and the Haudenosaunee peoples. Today, this meeting place is still home to many Indigenous people from across Turtle Island and we are grateful to have the opportunity to work and play here.

We acknowledge the financial support of the Canada Council for the Arts—which last year invested $153 million to bring the arts to Canadians throughout the country—the Ontario Arts Council (OAC), Ontario Creates, and the Government of Canada for our publishing activities.

This play is dedicated to the children in Seaton Village, my neighbourhood in Toronto.

The Fractured Subject of Judith Thompson

During the extended six-week workshop in the spring of 1990 that transformed Judith Thompson's radio play A *Big White Light* into the first stage version of *Lion in the Streets* at the du Maurier World Stage Theatre Festival in June 1990, Judith Thompson the director would occasionally ask the stage manager, Nancy Dryden, to break the company and dim the light in the small back space at Toronto's Tarragon Theatre where the workshop was being held. While actors and others drank coffee and ran lines in the lobby, Judith Thompson the writer walked about alone in the darkened room, getting into the blood, as she says, of her characters. By the time the break was over she would present, with astonishing rapidity, new, remarkable, and quite unexpected passages of text, often replacing brilliant lines or even whole scenes that, however effective in themselves, were deemed to be expendable. Great lines, she says, are a dime a dozen.

Quite apart from her alacrity in cutting, Judith Thompson's process as a writer is consistent with her background as a graduate in English from Queen's University and from the acting program of the National Theatre School, and congruent with Tarragon Theatre's reputation as the home of poetic naturalism. Her own training as an actor no doubt reinforced Thompson's well-developed sense of characterization and her acute ear for dialogue, and Tarragon Theatre proved for almost two decades a congenial host for Thompson's writer-in-residency and a valued first producer for all of her plays from 1984 until 2006.

But if poetic naturalism, however evocative, were all she wrote, Judith Thompson would not have the reputation she does as the creator of disturbing and dislocating theatrical experiences. *Lion in the Streets*, like all her plays, betrays an abiding interest in psychological motivation, and evokes immediate empathy for characters who are conceived in depth. Unlike those in more conventionally naturalistic plays, however, the characters in *Lion in the Streets* tend to be fragmented and discontinuous, and they are rarely contained within a single, unified action or linear plot. They tend, too, to be represented self-consciously as constructs undergoing crises of subjectivity, struggling to bridge a persistent gulf between the self that speaks and the self represented in that discourse as the subject, the "I." As the characters struggle to construct a unified self through a narrative that will allow them to understand—or "comprehend"—their lives, the play's plot becomes the site of duelling, contradictory, and even mutually exclusive narratives—multiple actions that are disturbingly open and exploratory rather than comfortably closed. This seems to be the case on the level of character and individual scene, in which the often violent or disjunctive actions are matched by a radical uncertainty about what is "really happening," about whose point of view is "true," and under what circumstances. But it is also the case that the overall "relay" structure of the play resists closure, containment, and easy comprehension, as a character from each scene is carried forward to the next, catalyst to a new action. As Thompson said, during a panel discussion at the du Maurier World Stage, "I just couldn't cope with the idea of a huge body of narrative. . . I started to find that kind of narrative tedious, because your expectations are usually fulfilled." Replacing the unity of traditional linear narrative are the overarching but problematic presence of Isobel, the play's collage-like composite portrait of an urban neighbourhood in crisis and, in production, a multiplicity of associative visual and musical linking devices such as the act-ending dances and the evocative disk that featured above centre-stage in the original du Maurier World Stage and Tarragon productions.

Naturalistic drama traditionally relies on the creation of fully empathetic characters whose psychological crises—constructed by the plays as personal neuroses—precipitate conflicts in the action. These conflicts are resolved through a "reversal" in the play's central and linear plot, producing in the central character(s) a "recognition" of an already existing, "well-adjusted," and unified "self" whose problems have been explained as deviations from a hegemonic social "norm." The empathy created between character and audience in such plays in turn produces a cathartic release of potentially disruptive emotions in an audience that leaves the theatre satisfied—calm of mind, all passion spent. Such plays, then, serve to contain potential social and psychological unrest, to explain disturbances and dissatisfactions in terms of individual psychology, and by purging discontent to affirm the social and political status quo.

In the plays of Judith Thompson, and most clearly in *Lion in the Streets*, intense empathy with naturalistically conceived character functions quite differently: in spite of a presentation of character that is psychologically acute, nothing is explained away. As she remarked at the du Maurier World Stage panel session, "I don't want to write industrial plays that play to psychology classes." Thompson's characters experience a conflict between a self that is submissive to the inherited and hegemonic discursive practices of society and a self that is not synonymous with the subject of that discourse. The conflicts in *Lion in the Streets*, far from moving towards resolutions that leave characters and audiences satisfied that things must be as they are, present occasions for potential—and potentially redemptive—transformation. The audience is not allowed to settle comfortably into a single, consistent, or unified way of viewing or empathizing with the characters, to identify actor with character, to feel superior awareness to the characters, or to construct any but provisional narratives with which to contain and comprehend the action. And to the extent that the play invokes closure, it does so without authority; that is, it invites the audience to make sense, to take responsibility for the meanings and for the world that its members individually construct from their own distinct subject positions. At the conclusion of *Lion in the Streets*, the apotheosis of Isobel is nevertheless redemptive, not as a logical, natural, or inevitable outcome of the play's actions, but as an active exercise of will—or even faith—on the part of an audience that is urged to "take your life. I want you all to have your life."

Lion in the Streets is a profoundly disruptive, socially subversive, and deeply religious play. It revisions traditionally phallo- and logocentric structures and languages, perverts the linearity of Aristotelian reversal and recognition, and replaces these with more radically contingent and consciously constructed shaping devices. And as in much feminist drama (as pointed out by Helene Keyssar in her book *Feminist Theatre*), the inevitability of reversal becomes in this play the possibility of transformation; recognition (of an already existing, unified subject) becomes the conscious selection of a subject position that is useful and meaningful in a particular context, and that allows audience members similar selection; and the experience of catharsis becomes the more unsettling but less enervating experience of fragmentation. Using the tools and intensity of psychological realism, *Lion in the Streets* dramatizes crises of subjectivity, and because its characters are characterized as constructs and presented as subjects in continuous process of construction, those crises are presented as providing for the possibility of change.

In spite of its realistic scenes of harrowing brutality and of ruthless emotional and intellectual honesty, the fracturing of subjectivity and revisioning of dramatic structure in *Lion in the Streets* are consistently used to insinuate the possibility of choosing and achieving "grace." And while the playwright sees "truth" as a passive state of tension, something that "happens to you through not doing anything," she posits "grace" in her unorthodox theology as the product of active human will, including the wills of audiences: "Truth," she says in an interview with Judith Rudakoff in *Fair Play*, "is simply what is. . . Grace is something you achieve. Through work. And Grace is something you have to work and work at. It happens through penitence, through sight. Through seeing who you are and changing things."

—Ric Knowles, 1992, updated in 2015

Lion in the Streets was first produced as the inaugural Public Workshop Project at Tarragon Theatre, Toronto, in May 1990, with the following cast and creative team:

Isobel: Tracy Wright
Nellie, Laura, Christine, and Sherry: Jane Spidell
Rachel, Lily, Rhonda, Ellen, and Scarlett: Ann Holloway
Scalato, Timmy, George, David, Rodney, and Ben: Stephen Ouimette
Martin, Isobel's Father, Ron, Father Hayes, and Michael: Andrew Gillies
Sue, Jill, Joanne, and Joan: Maggie Huculak

Stage manager: Nancy Dryden
Workshop assistants: Urjo Kareda, Ric Knowles, and Andy McKim
Set and costume design: Sue LePage
Music: Bill Thompson

Lion in the Streets received its world premiere at the du Maurier Theatre Centre as part of the du Maurier World Stage Theatre Festival in Toronto in June 1990, with the same cast and the following creative team:

Director: Judith Thompson
Set and costume design: Sue LePage
Sound effects: Evan Turner
Lighting design: Steven Hawkins
Stage manager: Nancy Dryden
Production assistants: Urjo Kareda, Ric Knowles, and Andy McKim

Production manager: Martin Zwicker
Set construction: George Vasiliou
Wardrobe: Cheryl Mills
Properties: Mary Spyrakis
Apprentice assistant stage manager: Henry Bertrand

Note

Although Isobel is Portuguese in the published script, her ethnic background can be changed for each production—which would mean changing names and some of the language—but most importantly, she must remain "other."

Act I

The ghost of ISOBEL, *a ragged-looking nine-year-old Portuguese girl, runs around and around in a large circle to music, terrified of a remembered pursuer. She is, in fact, running from the man who killed her in this playground seventeen years before the start of the play. There are autumn leaves all over the playground, and the kids who approach her have large handfuls of them, which they throw at her. At this point* ISOBEL *does not know she is a ghost, but she knows that something is terribly wrong. She is terrified. She speaks to the audience.*

ISOBEL   Doan be scare. Doan be scare. *(turns to audience)* Doan be scare of this pickshur! This pickshur is niiiice, nice! I looove this pickshur; this pickshur is mine! *(gesturing behind her)* Is my house, is my street, is my park, is my people! You know me; you know me very hard! I live next house to you, with my brother and sisters, Maria, Luig, Carla, and Romeo—we play; we play with your girl, your boy—you know me; you know me very hard. But. . . when did tha be? Tha not be now!

3

Tha not be today! I think tha be very long years ago. I think I be old. I think I be very old. Is my house but is not my house; is my street but is not my street; my people is gone; I am lost. I am lost. I AM LOOOOOOOOOST!!

Four children—two girls and two boys—laugh and approach ISOBEL.

NELLIE   Take a bird, why doncha?

RACHEL   Go back with the nutties to the nuttyhouse!

SCALATO   She looks like a crazy dog!

MARTIN   *(barks)* Hey!

They all bark.

ISOBEL   Peoples! Peoples, little boy, little girl peoples! Hey!

ISOBEL walks towards them.

MARTIN   What's she doin?

NELLIE   She's coming over here!

RACHEL   She's gonna get us!

ISOBEL   You, girl, you help to me. I am lost, you see! You help!

NELLIE   She smells.

RACHEL   You should dial 911 so the police could help you.

SCALATO   Where do you live?

MARTIN   With all the other pork and cheese west of Christie Street?

RACHEL   Martin, that's not nice.

ISOBEL   (overlapping) Portuguese, Portuguese, yes. . . I catch a bus! Is there a bus, bus maybe? To take me to my home? You know a bus?

SCALATO   No buses here.

ISOBEL   Yeah, bus right here, bus right here, number ten, eleven. I take with my mother to cleaning job; where this bus?

SCALATO   I said there's no buses here, you ugly little SNOT.

ISOBEL   (points) You! YOU bad boy; you bad boy say Isobel, BAD.

SCALATO   Why don't you get your ugly little face outta here, snot?

MARTIN   Snotface!

ISOBEL   Shut up, boy, shut up. I kill you; I kill you, boy.

SCALATO   Hey, she's gonna kill me!

RACHEL   She's a witch.

        ISOBEL tosses rocks at them.

MARTIN   She's throwin rocks! Hey, she's throwin rocks!

NELLIE   STOP IT.

RACHEL   Stop throwin rocks or we'll tell the police!

ISOBEL   You BAD boy; you BAD. I will kill you!

SCALATO   *(jumping off and attacking her)* You just try it, you goddamned faggot!! Faggot! Faggot!!

        SCALATO is hitting her.

ISOBEL   *(growling like a dog)* G-r-r-r-r-r. G-r-r-r-r-r.

        They circle one another.

MARTIN   What's she doing?

NELLIE   I don't like her.

        ISOBEL and SCALATO scrap and the others join in. SUE, a thirty-eight-year-old woman in a grey sweatsuit walking home from a meeting, spies the fight and rushes up.

SUE   Hey! Hey hey hey, stop that right now!

          SUE pries them apart.

          HEY! Listen! What is going on??

ISOBEL   I KILL YOU, BOY!

SCALATO   She started it!

MARTIN   She was throwing rocks at us!

RACHEL   She's crazy.

          ISOBEL leaps towards SCALATO. SUE catches her and falls to the ground.

SUE   Little girl? Little girl!

ISOBEL   *(overlapping)* I kill that stupid boy.

SCALATO   She started it, lady.

MARTIN   I'm getting out of here.

SCALATO   Me too.

NELLIE & RACHEL	Wait for me!!
SCALATO	You chicken, Martin! You suck!
ISOBEL	I kill that stupid boy!

Beat.

I no like those boys.

SUE	I'm sorry if they hurt you.
ISOBEL	They no want play with me. Why they no want play with me? Why all the kids no want play with Isobel? Ha?
SUE	Ohhh. . . sometimes kids are just. . . mean that way, Isobel. When I was little kids were mean like that to me once.
ISOBEL	Kids? Mean no play to you?
SUE	That's right. We had just moved to a new town— Cornwall actually, near Montreal? Well my sisters and I went for a walk around the neighbourhood and these big boys on bikes started firing arrows at us.
ISOBEL	Boys on bikes?

SUE	That's right, just like those nasty boys!
ISOBEL	Nasty boys, to you, too! Mean to you!!
SUE	That's right. And those arrows, they hurt! They really hurt!! And I was the oldest so I told my sisters, "Just cry, just start to cry and then maybe they'll feel sorry for us," so we all started to cry.
ISOBEL	Cry.
SUE	But you know what? It didn't work! They kept shooting those arrows anyways. They were just mean.
ISOBEL	Mean boys shoot arrows. Haaah!
SUE	AND suddenly, a bigger boy, about sixteen, came along and made them stop, and you know, he was like an angel, to us, an angel who came down from the sky on his big blue bicycle. I've never forgotten that.
ISOBEL	Never forgetting.
SUE	Nope. I guess I'm your helper today.
ISOBEL	Helper.
ISOBEL'S FATHER	*(on porch)* Hey! Is-o-bel.

SUE	Isobel, is that your father?
ISOBEL	Father. My father. *Eu pensava que té tinha perdedo!*
ISOBEL'S FATHER	*(ordering* ISOBEL *to go around to the back door) Vai pela porta das traseiras.*
SUE	Hello.

ISOBEL'S FATHER *grunts.*

My name is Sue Winters, and I don't know if you're aware of it, but some of the boys in the neighbourhood have been, well, I'd say doing some not very nice teasing of your daughter. I just. . . thought. . . you might. . .

ISOBEL'S FATHER *goes in, slamming the door.*

Poor man probably works all day in construction and then all night as a janitor in some Bay Street office building. What a life.

SUE *exits.*

ISOBEL	My father? My father is not there. My father is dead. Yes, was killed by a subway many many years; it it breathed very hard push push over my father; push over to God. Hi my father.

Music. Lights come up just a bit. SUE *is in her son* TIMMY's *room, in the dark.* TIMMY *is in bed.* ISOBEL *watches.*

SUE   And so the giant starfish saved the drowning boy.

TIMMY   What was the starfish's name?

SUE   The starfish's name? Uh. . . Joey. It was Joey.

TIMMY   Mummy? Why isn't magic true? I want magic to be true.

SUE   Well. It is true, in a way, it. . .

TIMMY   No it's not. It's not true. And ya know what else?

SUE   What, darling?

TIMMY   I think tonight's the night.

SUE   That what, Tim?

TIMMY   That we're all gonna die. Tonight's the night we're gonna die.

         Music. A dinner party around a table. ISOBEL *is there, invisible. The conversation is simultaneous.*

LAURA   There was nothing to do! Nothing to bloody do but sing in the church choir!! And go to baked-bean suppers!! The snow at one point was actually up to the second-floor window.

BILL   No, she had the gall to ask my male students to "please leave the room" for her senior seminar. She did "not wish to be dominated by men." Where did that leave me, I asked her?

LILY   No, no no, you have to pat the dough, pat it for ohh a good five minutes, then put it in the micro-wave for one, then take it out, then pat it again.

GEORGE St. Paul said, "We are as vapour." What is it? Like "vapour vanisheth" or—something. "We are no more." So I got up this notion of Martians—being these—wisps of vapour. . . No, you see, your prob-lem is you want the aliens to be like you; you are anthropomorphizing; you. . .

LAURA   That's so boring. That's so knee-jerk boring.

BILL   And she launched into the most savage tirade—

        SUE rushes in, dressed in her sweatsuit and sneak-ers. Everyone turns and freezes, except BILL, who continues to talk until SUE's third "Bill."

SUE   Bill. . . Bill. . . Bill!! We have to talk!

BILL   Sue! Hi! Who's with the boys?

SUE   Mum came over. Bill, I need to talk, NOW.

LAURA   Would you like a drink, Sue? We have. . .

GEORGE   Yeah, come in and sit down. . .

SUE   No, no thank you, I just. . . want to talk to my
           husband.

ISOBEL   My helper, Suuuuusan!

BILL   Oh—okay, Sue, I'll just finish this conversation.
           Anyway—

SUE   He thinks he's going to die.

BILL   Who?

SUE   Timmy! Your son! He—

BILL   What, did he say that tonight? Oh, that's just
           kids, he's—

SUE   BILL, come home, your son is very depressed; his
           father is never there; why are you never never. . .

BILL   Sue, PLEASE, we'll talk about it later, okay? So as
           I was saying, Laura. . .

SUE   Come with me.

BILL   I'll come in a while. I'll just finish this conversa-
              tion, and then I'll come, okay?

SUE   YOU COME WITH ME NOW!

BILL   Sue.

SUE   Bill, I need you, please; why won't you come?

BILL   Why won't I come? Why won't I come? Because. . .

              He walks over to the others.

              I'm. . . not. . . I am not coming home tonight.

SUE   Bill! Stop it, this is private—

BILL   It is not private, Sue; nothing we do is private,
              for Christ's sake; you tell your friends everything;
              they all—know everything—about us, don't they?
              How many times we had sex in the last month.

LAURA   I don't think that's true, Bill.

GEORGE   I haven't heard anything.

SUE   Bill, I think you're being very unreasonable.

              *There is an awkward pause in which BILL and
              SUE lock eyes.*

LAURA   (to LILY and GEORGE) Well, it's a lovely night out
         there. Why don't the three of us go for a walk?

BILL   No.

SUE   You stay and finish up that wonderful looking
         chocolate pâté, Laura; I'm sure you spent a lot
         of time on it. I'll just get Bill's coat and we'll go
         on home.

BILL   There is. . . somebody else, Sue. And I will be
         going home with her.

GEORGE   I think we've all had a little too much to drink;
         why don't we just. . .

SUE   Don't worry, guys; this isn't real. He's just drunk.
         He's just trying to scare me because we had this
         argument about the new sofa— Come on, honey,
         let's go home. Who is it? Who is it, Bill? She's not
         here, is she? You didn't, you didn't bring her to my
         neighbours', OUR friends' dinner party, to which I
         was invited. Laura! Laura, for God's sake.

LILY   It's me.

         SUE laughs.

         Why do you think I'm joking?

         SUE looks at LILY, then looks at BILL.

SUE	Bill??
BILL	This is—Lily.
LILY	How do you do, Susan?
SUE	Don't you call me by my name, you FAT!! Please, I don't think you know what you're doing. This is not just me, this is a family, a family—we have two children.
LILY	I'm sorry.
SUE	Bill, you are not leaving your children.
BILL	Sue, please.
SUE	YOU TOOK A VOW! In a CHURCH in front of a priest and my mother and your mother and your father and you swore to LOVE and honour and cherish till DEATH US DO PART, TILL DEATH US DO PART, BILL; it's your WORD. Your WORD.
BILL	I am breaking my word.
SUE	No!
BILL	YOU turned your back on me!! You you—look at you in that. . . sweatsuit thing; you're not—I mean look at her, really, you're, you're, you're a kind of. . . cartoon now, a. . . cartoon mum a. . . with

your daycare meetings and neighbourhood fairs;
you know what I mean, Laura! Your face is a drawing—your body—lines. The only time, the only
time you are alive, electric again is. . . when you
talk on the phone, to the other mums; there's a
flush in your face, excitement, something rushing
through your body; you laugh, loudly; you make
all those wonderful female noises; you cry; your
voice, like. . . music, or in the park, with Timmy
and John, while they cavort with the other children at the drinking fountain, spraying the water
and you talking and talking with all the moth-
ers, storming, storming together your words like
crazy swallows, swooping and pivots and. . . land-
ing. . . softly on a branch, a husband, one of us
husbands walk in and it's like walking into. . . a
large group of. . .

LILY   You see, I love. . . his body, Sue. I mean, I really
love it. I love to suck it. I love to kiss it—his body
is my God, okay? His body—

    SUE slaps LILY twice.

SUE   YOU. . . DON'T LIVE ON THIS STREET. You don't
belong in this neighbourhood.

    LILY contains herself from slapping SUE back.

Where did you meet this. . . woman? On the
street?

BILL starts to try to answer.

In a house of prostitution? I demand to know—

LILY   I had sex with him on the telephone, Susan, many many times.

SUE   That is a disgusting. . . lie.

LILY   Come on, Suzy, don't you remember? You caught him a couple of times, on the downstairs phone with his pyjamas around his ankles; he told me!

BILL   Hello.

LILY   Hi there.

BILL   You got back to me quickly.

LILY   Fucking right.

BILL   Fucking right.

LILY   Your voice makes me crazy.

BILL   My voice.

LILY   I'm wet, Bill, wet just from hearing your voice.

BILL   What are you wearing?

LILY   Black silk underwear, red spiked heels, black
          lace bra.

BILL   Yeah? And what do you want? What do you want?

LILY   You know what I want.

BILL   Oh baby, baby.

LILY   I want you all night long.

BILL   Yes, yes, oh yes! Yes! Yes!

LILY   Oh, Bill!

SUE   BILLLLLLLLLLLLLLLLLLLLLL!!!!!!!

          SUE physically attacks LILY.

          Aghhhh! Listen, you, if you take my husband
          away from me and my children I will. . . kill
          you. I will I will. . . come when you are sleep-
          ing and I will pull your filthy tongue out of
          your filthy mouth. And then I will. . . feed it to
          our cat.

BILL   Susan.

SUE   *(forced laugh)* I didn't mean that, I really didn't.
          I'm sorry, everybody, this is all just so ridicu-
          lous and embarrassing and I'm sure we'll all

laugh about it someday—I KNOW we will—but um. . . Bill? Won't you just. . . give me a chance? To show you? That I can? Be sexy? 'Cause I can, you know, much much more so than THAT creepy shit. . . don't you remember? Don't you remember before we were married how you loved to watch me dance? Come on, you did! Remember remember that wedding, Kevin and Leslie's? I wore that peach silk that you loved so much, that dress drove you crazy! And after after the wedding we were in that room in the Ramada Inn over the water and I danced? You lay on the bed and you just. . . watched me; you loved it, I. . . whooshed whooshed in that dress, back and forth to this thing on the radio, back and oooh and back and you were laughing and and *(laughs)* and whoosh.

The music beats louder, filling the room, and SUE begins a slow striptease.

And whoosh. . . and. . . close to you, you're hard. . . and far away and. . . turn. . . and whooosh. . . and. . . let. . . my. . . hair. . . down. . . you—love my hair whoosh and. . . zipppper. . . whoooo down so slowwwww turn and turn. . . you watching, laying on the bed and ease. . . off my shoulders, you love my shoulders, elegant ohhh, Billy, and down. Over my body the soft silky down and whooooooooooooooooo whooooooooooo, Billy.

Take me home, Billy, take me home and let's make mad, passionate love! Please.

BILL and LILY leave. GEORGE and LAURA pick up SUE's clothing and bring it to her. LAURA dresses her.

LAURA   Honey, I'm sorry.

SUE   Aghh, don't feel sorry for me, it's fine, everything will be fine because. . . his colon cancer's gonna come back, don't you think? Dr. Neville said he had a sixty-forty chance it will. And she'll drop him, for sure, don't you think? And he will let me nurse him; I will. . . feed him broth, with a spoon, like I did my mum, and I will hold, I will hold his sweet head in my chest till till his lips are black and his eyes. . . like bright dead stars and he is dead and I will stay, I will stay with his body, in the hospital room, because I did love that body. . . oh I did *love— that—body* once.

ISOBEL   Susan, Susan, Susan. The boy with the arrow ha *killed* you, ha? Where's your helper now? Oh, Susan, you can't help me now, you can't take me home. *(to the audience)* Hey! Who gonna take me home? You? You got a car? What kinda car you got? Trans Am? What about bus tickets? You got bus tickets? C'mon. Come on. COME

ON. SOMEBODY. What I'm sposed to do, ha? Who gonna take me home? Who gonna take me home?

> ISOBEL *finds a watching place. A few hours later, at* LAURA *and* GEORGE's, LAURA *clears the table.*

LAURA Poor Suzy. Poor poor Suzy.

GEORGE *(half asleep)* Yeahh. Chee.

LAURA God, that is the worst thing I have ever seen happen to anybody.

> GEORGE *and* LAURA *laugh hysterically and imitate* SUE *in the previous scene.*

GEORGE Whoosh! That peach silk, oh baby, take me home.

LAURA Take me home, Bill. Let's make mad, passionate love. *(stops imitating* SUE*)* I don't know, I mean I know she needs a friend badly. I am her friend; I mean, I love her. George, how can you laugh? This is important. If she calls me tomorrow, what should I say? I'm just going to say, I'm going to say, "SUZY? I feel really badly for you and I think you're a wonderful person but you will have to look somewhere else for—"

GEORGE Nice.

LAURA   GEORGE, you KNOW—

GEORGE   You always say she's your best friend, Laura, "My
             BEST—"

LAURA   She is! But, George, are you forgetting Maria? I
             had a nervous breakdown because of that woman
             and her problem; how could you FORGET?

GEORGE   I was on the book tour, Loo.

LAURA   I told you about it a hundred times; how could
             you forget?

GEORGE   I was on the book tour—Loo.

LAURA   George, you are so insensitive, I can't believe this.
             I told you about it one hundred times. How can
             you forget?

             GEORGE *grabs a tablecloth and wraps it
             around his head like a shawl and speaks in a
             Portuguese accent.*

GEORGE   How could I forget, how could I forget?

LAURA   George.

GEORGE   Looka this. Me? I donta forget nothing.

LAURA	George, I'm going to bed. Molly gets up in two hours and it's always me that gets up with her of course.

She walks around the circle.

GEORGE/ MARIA	LAURA.

Now he speaks as MARIA, ISOBEL's *mother.* ISOBEL *recognizes her.*

LAURA	George! Come to bed.

GEORGE/ MARIA	LAURA.

LAURA	Maria.

MARIA	I am. . . so sorry to be coming to your house, maybe you busy, I don't know—

LAURA	No, no, please come in, Maria, I'm just—reading the paper; the kids are at school and—

MARIA starts shaking violently and keening. She looks like she is in shock.

Maria?. . . uh. . . Maria? Are you all right? You look—why don't you sit down. Here. Sit down. Can I get you a drink of water?

> MARIA *starts to keen with grief, quite quietly.*

MARIA   Eeeeeeee. . .

LAURA   Maria? Maria. . . are you all right? Maria, Maria please tell me. . . what's. . .

MARIA   . . . I think. . . I think. . . Antonio—

LAURA   Your husband? Something happened to your husband?

> MARIA *continues to keen.*

It's okay, Maria, you don't have to tell me if you don't—

MARIA   Five o'clock in the morning, I cook: smelt and three scramble eggs, nice bread, coffee. For Antony must work long day, construction on highway, long day in the sun; he come from his shower to kitchen, but he don't want. He got a rat in his stomach that day he say, make a joke, don't want my cooking, eat a little bit a bread and just small glass of milk and he go, catch his subway. I fold. I fold clothes, one pile for Antony, one pile for me, one for Maria, Romeo, ISOBEL and Luig; my hands fold the clothes but my. . . *(gesture indicating self or soul)*

LAURA   Sure, you go on automatic—I—

MARIA   Like I fold myself too, and I go in his body, maybe,
          you know, his. . . hand to wipe off his face when
          he hot and too sweat; I am there.

          *She walks operatically downstage and delivers
          the rest of the speech, which should be like
          an aria.*

          I am foldin a light sheet of blue then and sudden
          I can see through his eye, am at subway, in him;
          he stands on the platform, is empty, empty, and
          I am his head, circles and circles like red birds
          flying around and around. I am his throat, tight,
          cannot breathe enough air in my body—the floor,
          the floor move, and sink in, rise up, rise like a
          wall, like a killin wave turn turn me in circles
          with teeth in circles and under and over I fall!

          ISOBEL *falls on an imaginary track in front of
          her mother.*

          I fall on the silver track nobody move—I hear-
          ing the sound. The sound of the rats in the
          tunnel, their breath like a basement these dark
          rats running running towards me. I am stone, I
          am earth, cannot scream, cannot move, the rats
          tramp. . . trample my body flatten and every bone
          splinter like. . .

          We *hear the sound of a strong wind as the
          sugar meeting is being set up on the stage.*

> *By the end of the wind,* LAURA *is at her table,*
> *addressing the meeting.*

LAURA   Good evening, everybody.

GEORGE   Good evening.

RON   Hi, Laura.

LAURA   I, uh, might as well get straight down to business.
            As head and sole member of the menu research
            committee, I have spent some three weeks
            doing. . . a great deal. . . of. . . research, and even
            a little detective work. . .

> RON *and* GEORGE *are talking to one another.*

            . . . and I would like to make my presentation
            tonight without too much interruption, thank you.

GEORGE   Go for it.

RON   No problem.

LAURA   POINT ONE. Sugar: I strongly recommend that
            we make a concerted effort to eradicate all sugar
            from the children's diet. Sugar is an overstimu-
            lant; sugar is empty calories; sugar rots. . .

RON   Uh, I have to say that, while I agree, sure, too much
            sugar is not a good thing, that once in a while. . .

LAURA	Would you let your four-year-old smoke "once in a while"?
	A murmur from the crowd.
RON	*(with a little laugh)* I don't really think you can equate. . .
	ISOBEL rises and walks into the meeting.
LAURA	Sugar is a known carcinogen, Ron. I have a study right here. . .
JILL	Lettuce is a known carcinogen, for God's sake!
ISOBEL	Hey! Boys! Girls! Looka this! I think tha they can't see me! They no see Isobel! Wha happen? Wha happen?
JILL	Okay, as chairperson, I say—let's cut the comments and raise our hands for questions. Laura? You want to go ahead?
LAURA	Yes, thank you, Jill. Uh. *(clears her throat)* It has come to my attention. . .
	GEORGE groans.
	Excuse me, I have to ask you why you groaned like that, George. Did I say something wrong?

JILL   George, penalty for groaning out of turn—just
                kidding.

GEORGE   No, no, I'm sorry, I just, I don't know, I just. . . have
                a kind of a hard time with "meeting. . . talk". . . "It
                has come to my attention."

LAURA   Well, I'm very sorry, George, if you have a better
                way of—

JILL   That was uncalled for, George, really.

RON   George, your mother's calling you.

                General laughter.

JILL   Let's let Laura continue, please, so we can get out
                of here. . .

ISOBEL   I think I invisible!

LAURA   Thank you, Jill. I have NOTICED—if you don't like
                "it has come to my attention"—I have noticed
                that in this nursery school they are. . . subtly, and
                I'm sure unwittingly, encouraging an addiction
                to sugar in our children.

RHONDA   Hey, that's not true.

LAURA   Rhonda, I'm SAYING it's not intentional. . .

RHONDA   The kids are not. . .

LAURA   PLEASE LET ME TALK.

JILL   Go ahead, Laura, please.

LAURA   I have noticed that sugar is used as a reward. If
             you're good we'll make cookies tomorrow. If you
             tidy up you get chocolate cake as a reward. You
             are creating. . . unwittingly, I concede, you are
             creating TOMORROW'S COKE ADDICTS. . . TO—

RHONDA   EXCUSE ME, I HAVE TO SAY THAT, AS THE CARE-
             GIVER, I RESENT THIS.

LAURA   Rhonda, I'm not accusing just you, I think you are
             fabulous with the kids, it's our whole society. . .

RHONDA   I am not creating drug addicts.

JILL   Rhonda, Laura does not mean any of this person-
             ally. I think that's. . .

LAURA   I'm saying it's a small step from sugar
             addiction to—

RON   Excuse me, I have to say, all food is sugar. . .

LAURA   REFINED SUGAR IS FAST-ACTING, RON, IT BURDENS
             THE PANCREAS.

GEORGE   I think you are taking this a little too seriously,
                Laura; we're just talking about a few cookies now
                and then, for heaven's sake.

LAURA   WE ARE TALKING ABOUT A LIFETIME ADDICTION
                AND I DON'T THINK IT SHOULD BE TAKEN LIGHTLY.

JILL   Laura, are you willing to listen to a response from
                Rhonda?

LAURA   Sure.

RHONDA   I would just. . . like to say that I also have done. . : a
                great deal of studying diet and menu and that, and
                I fully agree with Laura that sugar is. . . some-
                thing to be avoided, IF YOU CAN. Listen, if I'm
                giving the kids yogourt, they won't eat it without
                honey—they won't, so I figure, a bit of honey is
                worth getting the yogourt down 'em. . .

LAURA   BULLSHIT. THAT IS ABSOLUTE, UNADULTERATED
                BULLSHIT.

RHONDA   I beg your pardon, Laura?

LAURA   You don't know what you're saying, Rhonda.

RHONDA   If you don't trust me, Laura. . .

LAURA   Rhonda. . .

RHONDA   I do not encourage sugar. I do not hold it up as a
           reward, ever. I have never done that.

LAURA   You're lying, Rhonda.

RON   WAIT A MINUTE, HOLD ON JUST A. . .

LAURA   SHUT UP, RON. LISTEN. LISTEN TO ME, RHONDA. I
           FOUND OUT THAT JUST LAST FRIDAY, LAST FRIDAY,
           AS A REWARD, YOU TOOK SIX KIDS, INCLUDING MY
           TWINS, TO A DOUGHNUT SHOP. YOU TOOK THEM
           TO A DOUGHNUT SHOP AND BOUGHT THEM EACH
           A JELLY DOUGHNUT.

           I think I screamed for five minutes when the
           twins told me that; I just couldn't believe it. They
           started harassing me every five minutes, "Mum, if
           we're good, can we have a jelly doughnut?" I don't
           think they'd ever HEARD OF JELLY DOUGHNUTS
           BEFORE THAT!! I find it unconscionable, UNCON-
           SCIONABLE, that a jelly doughnut would be the
           sole purpose of an excursion.

RHONDA   Um, I can explain that. It was a Friday, right, and
           I happen to get severe cramps with my period,
           right? And I was very sick that day and the kids
           had bad bad cabin fever, well. . .

LAURA   (overlapping) And the Friday before that it was
           Popsicles, Rhonda. I'm not blaming you, I'm
           saying you need to be re-educated. We all do.

Smelling the flowers is a reason to go for a walk, not getting a poisonous body-destroying drug. . .

RHONDA   LET MEEEEE TALLLLLK. LET ME TALK LET ME TALLLLLLLLLLLLK!! I feel. . . nailed to the wall by you, lady, nailed right to the fucking wall. I have to say and something else I have to say is that I think you are. . . are very. . . inconsiderate. . . of feelings! I brought up two kids on what I feed your kids, and they turned out just fine, are you telling me what I feed my kids isn't good enough for your kids? You know, the funny thing is, Laura, you may be a bitch on wheels, but lookin at all the rest of you—Laura? at least you're honest you are. Youse others, what you're thinkin is. . . it really doesn't matter what they get at the daycare, the real learning is at home, that's where youse teach your kids to become— huh. Here I am saying "youse." I haven't said that since I was a kid! That's how flustered I am—at home you teach your kids. . . to be. . . higher kind of people, higher kind of people don't eat Kraft slices and tuna casserole. I've seen that kind a laugh in your voices, all of you, when you say, "Oh, they had *tuna casserole*." I seen—I have seen the roll in your eyes at the grace before meals, or the tidy-up song, or the stars we give out for citizen of the week. You think, "Oh well, the kid is happy, well cared for, we can undo all that and we can make the kids high people like ourselves, better people, more better people than the poor

little teacher who reads ROMANCE." Yes, yes, JILL
MATHINS, I saw you showin my book, my novel,
to RON there and Cathy and havin a big giggle.
You think I didn't see that? You think the books
you read are deeper, more. . . higher, well it's the
same story, don't you see that? What's makin me
cry in my book is, when ya come right down to
it, is exactly the same thing that's makin you cry
in your book. Oh yes, oh yes, and I'll tell you
something, I'll tell all of you I GREW UP ON THAT.
I grew up on jelly doughnuts and butter tarts,
and chocolate ice cream, and I happen to think
they're a wonderful thing. I happen to agree with
the mice and the cockroaches and the horses and
birds that treats are a wonderful thing. You need
treats; you need treats in this life. Each bit of a
treat can wipe out a nasty word, every bite of a
jelly doughnut cleans out your soul—it is a gift
from GOD, a wonderful gift from GOD, and I for
one. . . I for one. . . I. . . for. . . your eyes, eh? Your
eyes are all the same colour and shape like a picture, a. . . freaky art picture, all the same in a row
like dark soldiers raisin your. . .

> ISOBEL *shoots everybody there except* RHONDA
> *with her finger. There are real gunshot sounds,*
> *even though* ISOBEL *is imagining this.*

ISOBEL   *(big laugh, then struts)* Rho-HONDA! Bebbe!
Beautiful belle! I have killed those dirty bas-
tards, babe. I have killed them dirty dead. I am

your harmy, Rhohonda! And you! You gonna take
me home!

> ISOBEL *falls and wraps herself around* RHONDA's
> *feet. Music. A restaurant.* DAVID *takes his place
> behind the bar. Another person is sitting alone
> at a table.* RHONDA *and her friend* JOANNE *meet
> for drinks. They are laughing.* ISOBEL *watches.*

RHONDA   Oh man, is this Singapore Sling fantastic.

JOANNE   My Fuzzy Navel is warm. Hot!

RHONDA   SEND it back! We're paying through the teeth for
these drinks. Waiter, take this thing back!

JOANNE   No, I like it this way; honest, Rhonda, I do.

DAVID   Is there a problem with your cocktail?

JOANNE   No no no no, please. . .

DAVID   I could take it back—

JOANNE   No.

RHONDA   Are you sure?

JOANNE   I'm sure.

DAVID   Okaaay.

RHONDA   Ohhh, Christ, I'd like to just sit and drink all after-
            noon, to tell you the truth.

JOANNE   I thought you quit heavy drinkin.

RHONDA   I did. I'm just. . . down in the dumps.

JOANNE   Why, ya on your time?

ISOBEL   Is this my home? This is not my home!

RHONDA   No no no, I get happy then, no, it's just. . . work.

JOANNE   Yeah, jeez, I'm glad I'm not workin, it made me
            crazy. What's goin on? The kids at the daycare
            gettin to ya?

RHONDA   No no, it's not the kids, the kids are great, it's the
            parents.

JOANNE   Uh-oh. That same B-I-T-C-H?

RHONDA   No, she was quite good this time, strangely
            enough—it's another one.

JOANNE   They all look like bitches to me in their leather
            pants. Stuck up, puttin their kids in hundred-
            and-fifty-dollar shoes. I looked at the price of
            them Nikes for kids—the other day when I picked
            you up I saw three of those kids had those shoes
            on. I couldn't believe my eyes.

RHONDA	Yeah, well, they're pretty well-off, but I don't hold that against them. I mean, who wouldn't be if they had the chance, right?
JOANNE	Well that's a good point, so. . .
RHONDA	We had this meeting, okay?
JOANNE	RHONDA. Excuse me!
RHONDA	What?
JOANNE	*(intake of breath)* . . . I don't know.
RHONDA	What do you mean?
JOANNE	I mean. . . no, I don't know.
RHONDA	Joanne.
JOANNE	I mean. . . oh God, I wasn't going to tell nobody—
RHONDA	You're pregnant again?
JOANNE	No no no no, if only, I. . .
RHONDA	JOANNE, I'M YOUR BEST FRIEND.
JOANNE	YOU'RE MY BEST FRIEND?
RHONDA	Yes, you know that!

JOANNE	THEN SWEAR ON YOUR MOTHER'S LIFE.
RHONDA	What?
JOANNE	That you will do what I'm gonna ask you.
RHONDA	Joanne, what is this?
JOANNE	Just. . . swear.
RHONDA	I'm not swearing on my mother's life without knowing what it is; she's got enough problems. . .
JOANNE	Okay, your husband s life.
RHONDA	Okay, I swear on the asshole's life. There. Now what?
JOANNE	You remember. . . I had this pain in my back?
RHONDA	Yeah, for the last few months, every time ya bend down.
JOANNE	SEARING pain, every time I moved. . .
RHONDA	. . . Okay. . .
JOANNE	Well, remember I told you I went to that specialist and he said he was gonna do some tests?
RHONDA	Right, uh-huh.

JOANNE   Well—

RHONDA   You gotta go in and have an operation and you
           want me to take your kids—no problem, of
           COURSE I'll take them, Jo, for God's—

JOANNE   (overlapping) No. No, I mean, you might have to
           take the kids but that's only. . . part of it.

RHONDA   Joanne, I really don't like guessing games.

JOANNE   Shadows. . . that's what they call them, and. . . it
           is. . . the very worst thing it could be, and
           the. . . kind, the kind is of the bone.

RHONDA   Oh boy.

JOANNE   Yeah.

RHONDA   (whispers) Jo. . .

JOANNE   Don't. . . don't touch me. I'll go hysterical. Please.

RHONDA   YOU. . . want a cigarette?

JOANNE   Yeah.

           RHONDA *lights one and gives it to* JOANNE.

           Ya know, I have to go to the bathroom, like, real
           bad, but I'm not gonna go, ya know why? 'Cause

every time. . . I sit down to pee I feel my whole life drainin out of me, just draining out with the pee, goin. . . outta me, into the water down in the pipes, and under the. . . friggin. . . GROUND. That's where I'll be, Rho, that's where I'm gonna. . . *(fights to regain her composure)* I'll come home with the groceries? Like after dark? And I'll see Frank and the kids through the window, in the livin room, right? Watchin TV, or drawing on paper, cuttin out stuff, whatever, and I'll stand on the porch and watch 'em, just. . . playing. . . on the floor, and I think. . . that's life, that's life goin on without me. It'll be just like that, only I won't be here with the groceries, I'll be under the ground, under the ground with my flesh fallin off a my face and I just can't take it. You know in that picture? That picture I had in my bedroom growing up?

RHONDA   UHH—

JOANNE   My aunt and uncle sent me that from England, the poster. It's OPHELIA, from this play by Shakespeare, right? And she, she—got all these flowers, tropical flowers, wildflowers, white roses, violets and buttercups, everything she loved and she kinda weaved them all together. Then she got the heaviest dress she could find. . . you know how dresses in the olden days were so long and heavy, with petticoats and that? And she got this heavy heavy blue dress, real. . . blue and then she wrapped all these pretty pretty flowers round and round her body, round her head, and her hair; she had this golden, wavy hair, long, and then she steps down the bank, and she lies, on her back, in the stream. She lies there, but the stream runs so fast she's on her back and she goes. It pulls her along so fast and she's lookin at the sky and the clouds, and she's singing little songs. "I'm lookin over a four-leaf clover"—and being pulled so fast by a clear, cold water, pulled along and she's not scared; she's not scared at all—she's calm, so happy! And just ever so slowly her dress gets heavier, right? Then, then, she gets caught on a stick, like a branch, of a willow tree, and her dress pulls her down, soft. She's still singin down deep deep deep to the bottom of the stream and with all these "fantastic garlands," these beautiful flowers all around her—"one's for the roses that blew down the lane"—she dies, Rhon, she dies. . . good. She dies good.

RHONDA   That's. . . something.

JOANNE   I want to die like that. But. . . I don't. . . want to do it all alone. I mean, I want you to help me, with the flowers, and with the dress, and my hair, I want you to make sure the willow branch is there, and the stream is right, and maybe. . . maybe that. . . Frank. . . sees I. . . wouldn't mind him seein. . . me in that stream, with the flowers, and the heavy blue dress. . . I wouldn't mind if you took maybe some pictures of me like that and

then you could have them printed and given out
at the funeral, something like that. . . just, you
know, two by four, colour, whatever, it's the one
thing that would make it all right—it's the one
thing. . .

RHONDA   I just. . . I don't know, Jo; you know I'd do anything
to make it all right. . .

JOANNE   Well this is what I want, Rhonda. It's really really
really what I want. Are you going to help me?

RHONDA   I uh—think you need to see a counsellor, Jo; you
know they have counsellors that. . . specialize
in these. . . situations. I'm surprised your doctor
didn't. . .

JOANNE   You think I'm crazy.

RHONDA   No no, Joanne, I just think that. . . your situation
is so hard that you are not quite yourself. I mean,
this is not. . . you. The Joanne I know is practi-
cal, she. . . you should believe in the treatments,
Jo. They do work sometimes—they really do—
and the Joanne I know would never ask a friend
to help. . . her. . . is one of the most thoughtful
people that I know, of other people. And how the
hell, how the hell do you think that I could live
with that after, eh?? I mean it's all very lovely and
that, your picture, in your room, but that's a picture, that's a picture, you dimwit! The real of it

would be awful, the stalks of the flowers would be chokin you, and the smells of them would make you sick, all those smells comin at you when you're feelin so sick to begin with, and the stream, well, if you're talking about the Humber River or any stream in this country you're talkin filth. In the Humber River you're even talkin sewage, Jo. You're talkin cigarette packages and used condoms and old tampons floating by. You're talking freezin; you'd start shakin from head to toe. You're talkin rocks gashin your head. You're talkin a bunch of longhairs and goofs on the banks yellin at you, callin you whorebag, sayin what they'd like to do to you. You're talkin. . . and where would you get a dress like that, eh? You'd never find the one in the picture, Jo, it'd be too tight at the neck and the waist. It'd be a kind of material that itches your skin. Even worse wet, drives you nut-crazy, the blue would be off, wouldn't look right; your shoes wouldn't match. You could never find the same colour, Joanne. You can't become a picture, do you know what I mean? I mean you can't. . . BE. . . a picture, okay?

> *They freeze.* ISOBEL *runs from her watching place, around the circle, screaming; she has realized, listening to* JOANNE, *that she is not lost, but dead, murdered seventeen years before.*

ISOBEL   AAHHHHHHHHHHHH!! I am dead! I have been bones for seventeen years, missing, missing; my face in the TV and newspapers, posters, everybody lookin for, nobody find. I am gone; I am dead; I AM DEADLY DEAD! Down! It was night, was a Lion, roar!! With red eyes: he come closer *(silent scream)* come closer *(silent scream)* ROAR tear my throat out ROAR tear my eyes out. . . ROAR I am kill! I am kill! I am no more!

Music.

(to JOANNE) We are both pictures now. WHO WILL TAKE US? WHO WILL TAKE US TO HEAVEN, HA?

> *Lights down. Cathedral bells ring. DAVID is outside, walking down the street.*

DAVID God, that customer dying of bone cancer. I didn't even want to touch her glass. I don't know she had that look—that dead look. I mean, I almost felt hostile.

ISOBEL *(inside the cathedral)* I WANT TO GO TO HEAVEN NOW!

> *She sees a life-size statue of the Virgin Mary and approaches it.*

Holy Mary Mother of God. Will you take Isobel to heaven now, please?

> *She lies at the base of the statue, her hand touching the statue's foot.*

DAVID   God that cathedral is beautiful. Funny, I've passed
                     it every day on my way out from work and I've
                     never really looked at it. Look at the stonework,
                     those *spires*—

                     He opens the church doors and enters. The
                     doors slam behind him.

                     Oh I love this, it's so. . . the air is so. . . holy it
                     IS. . . Look at those bird-bath things full of holy
                     water. I love it, it's so primitive.

                     He splashes some water on his face.

                     In the name of the Father. . . the Son, and
                     the Holy—

FATHER
HAYES   Good evening.

                     DAVID shrieks, startled. His shriek echoes.

                     It's all right, it's all right. Have you come for. . .

DAVID   Confession. I've come for confession. Eight thirty,
                     yes? I'm not too late, am I? See, I just finished
                     work, and. . .

FATHER
HAYES   Not too late, of course not.

	FATHER HAYES goes into his part of the confessional.
DAVID	*(to himself)* I guess just—God, I don't remember a THING about what to do!!
	We hear the wooden barrier being opened, and the priest begins the Latin prayer, which we hear in English.
FATHER HAYES	In the name of the Father, and the Son, and the Holy Spirit.
DAVID	*(overlapping)* Oh God, he's saying something—
FATHER HAYES	May the Lord be in your heart and help you to confess your sins with true sorrow. Let us listen to the Lord as he speaks to us: I will give them a new heart and put a new spirit within them; I will remove the strong heart from their bodies and replace it with a natural heart, so that they will live according to my statutes, and observe and carry out my ordinances; thus they shall be my people and I will be their God.
DAVID	*(overlapping)* I think it's Latin. Isn't that against Papal Law? I should report him to the Vatican and have him defrocked. Here goes nothing—

FATHER HAYES finishes the prayer.

AHH—FORGIVE ME FATHER, FOR I have sinned. It
has been. . . four weeks since my last confession.
These are my sins?. . . OKAY, told Barb I'd be there
last night for dinner with her and the niece and
nephew—didn't show up, didn't phone, nothing. Was in a mad PASH with my hockey player.
I was very cruel to Daniel Thursday, saw him at
Billy's—the club? And I don't know, the way he
was looking at me drove me CRAZY CRAZY; he was
mooning! Well I walked up to him and told him
to "Quit mooning. I'd rather see your hairy ass
than that pathetic face, face it!" I said, "Face it,
you old fag, you have been dumped—DUMPED!"
That was really mean; that's gotta be more than
a venial sin. AND THEN, then, yesterday, I walked
through a park? And I saw a large group of poor
children playing, and I just thought they were
trouble; I wondered why God had put them in
the world; really, isn't that unkind? THEN today
I saw a fat lady eating an ice-cream cone and
I said, I think quite audibly I said "disgusting,"
oh AND I did not stand up in the subway—the
incredibly packed subway—for a hugely pregnant
lady and her kid. I just didn't feel like it. Quite
the catalogue, eh? Oh, and another thing, I've
lied to you already. I haven't been to confession
in fifteen years—haven't stepped in a church in
fifteen years, just. . . did it on a whim, don't ask
me why. I was passing by on my way. . .

FATHER HAYES	AND you felt the hand of GOD?
DAVID	Well. . . it was just a whim—really. . .
FATHER HAYES	David.
DAVID	How do you know my name?
FATHER HAYES	David, I know your name better than I know my own.
DAVID	Wait a minute, wait a minute, I think maybe this is some odd coincidence because although my name is DAVID, I don't actually know you at all, so. . .
FATHER HAYES	There's nothing odd about it, David. You were an altar boy for me, two years, for two years you served, in 1957 and 1958 at St. Bernard's in Moncton, New Brunswick. Remember?
DAVID	Moncton? We were around there for a couple of years—
FATHER HAYES	You were a believer, David; the other boys were just forced into it by their parents. You believed in every statue, every—

DAVID	Father Hayes? You—are Father Hayes?
FATHER HAYES	I am.
DAVID	You're still alive?
FATHER HAYES	I think.
DAVID	But you were so old even way back then!
FATHER HAYES	Not really.
DAVID	I remember you now. I remember, you did look old, because you stooped, and you had white hair already, didn't you?
FATHER HAYES	Indeed, I was prematurely silver. . .
DAVID	Silver hair and. . . and. . . red eyes.
FATHER HAYES	I. . . suffered from allergies, hay fever. I'm sorry if it frightened you.
DAVID	I guess maybe it did frighten me a bit, Father, but you know how young boys are—

FATHER
HAYES   I am sorry, but, but. . .

DAVID   No no, I. . . look, I uh—

FATHER
HAYES   David, I want. . .

DAVID   . . . don't mean to be impolite, but I'd like you
             to be honest with me, sort of man to man. I. . . I
             always got the impression that you were looking
             at me much more than you looked at the other
             boys, am I right?

FATHER
HAYES   Well. . .

DAVID   I felt. . . I felt as though your eyes were devour-
             ing me.

FATHER
HAYES   No, no, no. . .

DAVID   No?? I'm gay, Father, you can be honest with
             me. I'll forgive you. I mean, you never actually
             did anything; you never even touched me; you
             just. . . looked. You kept looking at me—tell me,
             tell me the truth.

FATHER
HAYES   It was not what you think, no, no, please—

DAVID   Confess to me, Father, come on, come on. . .

FATHER
HAYES   I make my confessions on a regular. . .

DAVID   Have you confessed this sin?

FATHER
HAYES   No, no I haven't, but—

DAVID   God loves sinners who confess, Father; you taught
               me that. As long as you speak up and you're sorry
               as hell, you're okay, you still got your ticket to
               heaven, but you won't; you won't, Father, if you
               don't tell me; you'll wither in LIMBO! I suffered. I
               need you to tell me! CONFESS. . .

FATHER
HAYES   I'm due to a christening. I have to shave first,
               there's a big party, I—

DAVID   You would christen a baby with this sin, bobbing
               on the surface, bobbing? Confess, you son of a
               bitch. Con—

FATHER
HAYES   Forgive me, Father, for I have sinned.

DAVID   All right.

FATHER HAYES	I looked at you, David, because. . . I. . . because. . . I wanted. . . to. . . remember. . . you.
DAVID	Remember me?
FATHER HAYES	Because. . . of what was to happen, in the water: oh OH, when the day arrived, when the picnic came round, in July, that Canada Day picnic? I had a bad feeling. I had. . . a very bad feeling indeed. We all piled out of the cars: families, priests, nuns, altar boys, piled out and lugged all those picnic baskets to tables under trees. The grown-ups all fussed with food and drink while the kids, all of you children, ran ran in your white bare feet to the water, throwing stones and balls, and a warning sound, a terrible sound of deep nausea, filled my ears and I looked up and saw you, dancing on the water, and I saw a red circle, a red, almost electric circle, dazzling round and round like waves, spinning round your head and body. I thought, "Watch, watch that boy, on this day he will surely drown, he *will*." David, *I knew that you would die*. And all because of the chicken. The twenty-nine-pound chicken brought there by Mrs. Henry grown on her brother's farm. Everyone had talked and talked about that chicken, who would carve that chicken. Mrs. Henry took it out and you skipped along the shore. She laid it on the table, "FATHER HAYES, YOU GO

AHEAD AND CARVE, AND DON'T MAKE A MESS OF
IT OR YOU WON'T SEE ME AT MASS NEXT SUNDAY."
Everyone laughed laughed, the men, the men
drinking beer, watching me, sure they're thinking,
"Watch him carve like a woman." Most men hate
priests—you know this is a fact—I could see them
thinking cruel thoughts under hooded eyes and
practised grins; my sin was the sin of pride! The
sin of pride, David. I started to carve, didn't want
to look up, lest I wreck the bird. You see, at that
moment that chicken was worth more, indeed
worth more. . . than your LIFE, David. I SHUT
OUT the warning voice and I—carved. I carved
and carved and ran into trouble, real trouble. I
remember thinking, "Damn, how does any person
do it; it's a terrible job." People behave as if it's
nothing, but it's terrible. I kept at it; I wouldn't
give up, I wouldn't look up till I'd finished, and
I finished carving, and I had made a massacre.
The men turned away the women. . . murmured
comfort, and before I looked up I had a hope, a
hard hope, that you were still skipping on the
rocks and shouting insults to your pals. All hands
reached for chicken and bread, potato salad, chocolate cake. I looked, I looked up and your hand
from the sea, your hand, far away, was reaching,
reaching for me far away. . . oh no! I ran, and
tripped, fell on my face, ran again. I could not
speak, ran to the water and shouted as loud as I
could, but my voice was so tiny; I saw your hand,
ran to the fisherman close. He wasn't home; his

fat daughter and I, in the skiff, not enough wind, no wind, paddling paddling, you a small spot, nothing, then nothing. The sun burns our faces, our red red faces.

DAVID

And I. . . was. . . never found?

FATHER
HAYES

And now. . . you have come!! You have finally come!!

DAVID

And what have I come for?

> *FATHER HAYES is sleeping.*

Uh. . . Father? Uh, listen. . . I'm sorry. I'm sorry but I never died. You got the wrong guy. I knew you. . . some other time—I mean, shit, I wish I had died. I only wish, it would have made my life so much more interesting. . . I grew up; I grew up. Listen, if I had drowned in the sea, in Moncton, New Brunswick, a beautiful, perfect young boy, if I was. . . pulled by the sea, if I reached and was lost, and all those people felt this loss, a loss all their lives, mother, father, brothers and sister, friends, a dark ache, somewhere in their chest for what could have been, they could all imagine, you see, what could have been, Father. Father? I forgive you; I forgive you, Father. It was nice on the water, you know? It was neat, so calm, as I slipped underneath. I wasn't scared, I'll tell ya. I wasn't scared a bit. The water was so. . . nice!!

> *Music.* ISOBEL *dances, joined by the cast one by one until they are all dancing fully. The cast dance off one by one, leaving* ISOBEL *alone, who freezes. Blackout.*

Act II

> *Sounds of kids playing in a park. A group of mothers chat.* ISOBEL *watches.*

CHRISTINE   How's your pregnancy going, dear?

> *A lion roars.*

ISOBEL   I hear the LION. I hear the Lion ROAR!!

ELLEN   Wonderful! I finally feel. . . good for something. LEO, SHARE IT. Share it, please.

CHRISTINE   Not me. NOT me. When I was pregnant I felt as useful as a cow. A large, stupid. . .

ELLEN   Christine!!

CHRISTINE   EMMA! Five more minutes, honey! Mummy's got to go to work! Well, considering I despised the man whose child I was carrying—

ELLEN   I suppose that would. . . alter things—GOOD CATCH, Leo!

SUE   Hi guys. Timmy, just five minutes. Remember,
              your father's coming to get you at five.

CHRISTINE   Sue, I love that blouse! Really suits you!

ELLEN   Gorgeous!

SUE   Thank you. I'm organizing a bake sale, if you can
              believe it, for the community centre over on Ash
              Street. PLEASE say you'll bake, or sell tickets, even
              a promise to buy—

ISOBEL   I must tell these peoples; I must tell them now!

ELLEN   Forget me, I'm a diabetic! I can't even look at the
              stuff.

SUE   Tim! Why don't you try the swing? You love
              swings.

CHRISTINE   Okay, put me down for fudge brownies, if my kids
              don't eat them first.

              GEORGE enters with a kid's bicycle.

              George! How's the book going?

GEORGE   Well, well, very well indeed!! And how's the
              busiest freelancer in town? Bradley, don't push
              so hard!

CHRISTINE   Overworked and underpaid.

GEORGE   What else is new?

>   *RON enters.*

>   Ron! Why aren't you at your office?

ELLEN   We're telling!

GEORGE   Good. Bradley!

SUE   Tim? Why don't you try the swing?

CHRISTINE   RON, did you get my note? EMMA, PUT IT BACK!

RON   Yes, I did, I I I—

ISOBEL   *(hitting them)* Shut up, boy! Shut up, girl! I say, I say it's time!! He's in the streets. Get them out, he's in the streets. Save your children, take their hand, take their leg.

SUE   Isobel! I saw this girl before, she—

ISOBEL   I say shut up! I say LISTEN TO ME NOW! Can you no hear? Listen! Can you nooo—

>   *All freeze except SUE, who crosses slowly towards the children.*

SUE   Timmy?

ISOBEL   *(goes to her)* The Lion is here, in your streets. He
             is trying to kill you, to kill all of your children. He
             really really is.

                        *She picks up a great crooked stick that she will
                        carry until she says "I love you" to* BEN *in the
                        final scene.*

             Watch me! *(laughs)* I am your HARMY! *(laughs)*
             I am your SAINT! I am your HARMY! Watch me,
             watch me. *(a war cry)* I WILL KILL THE LION NOW!!

                        Thunderstorm as SUE *shouts "*TIMMMYY!!*" and
                        the others ad lib to their children. All exit. A
                        kid's bike is left on stage. Blackout. Lights up
                        on* CHRISTINE *walking towards* SCARLETT'S *base-
                        ment apartment, tracked by* ISOBEL.

ISOBEL   This girl, Christine—Christine, this girl, SHE will
             take me to the Lion, yes, for she. . . she is very
             hard. Harrrrd. HARRRRRRRD!!

CHRISTINE   116 Carlisle. Lord what a stench. What could
             that be?

                        CHRISTINE *knocks on the door.*

SCARLETT   Come in!

CHRISTINE   Scarlett Deer?

SCARLETT   That's my name, don't wear it out, has to last a lifetime!!

CHRISTINE   I'm Christine Pierce from the *Telegraph*. We talked on the phone.

SCARLETT   Have a seat.

CHRISTINE   Thank you. Nice place.

SCARLETT   What, this hole? Sorry if it stinks. I cooked chicken today an ever since I ate it I been fartin up a storm. Dead chicken farts, that's what my brother always said.

CHRISTINE   Scarlett, I don't have a lot of time, so is it all right if I ask you some questions?

SCARLETT   Sure, how does it feel to be an ugly geek? Fine, thank you, fuck you very much.

CHRISTINE   Scarlett, advanced multiple sclerosis is a serious handicap. Don't you feel that living on your own is dangerous?

SCARLETT   Would you like to live in a freak house?

CHRISTINE   Well, Scarlett, I—

SCARLETT   Freedom—freedom, girl. I'd rather fuckin rot on
             the floor of my own home than be well-fed and
             cared for in a freak house.

CHRISTINE   What you're saying, then, is that above all things
             you cherish freedom. That you would rather risk—

SCARLETT   Once when my volunteers were sick? All of 'em
             were sick, right? And I just wanted to see what the
             hell I would do? I lay in my own shit and piss for
             three days.

CHRISTINE   Good Lord, what—

SCARLETT   I coulda phoned somebody, my parents live down
             the street, but I just wanted to see. . . I wanted to see
             how long I'd survive; I wanted to see if I could do it.

CHRISTINE   Well, who did you eventually—

SCARLETT   My mother, my poor mother. And it makes me
             sick, sick, because what will I do when they die?
             They're old, you know, they're gonna die soon.

CHRISTINE   What will you do?

SCARLETT   I'll die on the floor in my shit and piss.

CHRISTINE   Scarlett, do you have any hobbies? That is, what do
             you do between volunteers? Do you have favourite
             soap operas or game shows, or—

SCARLETT   I screw my brains out.

CHRISTINE   *(a weak laugh)* No, seriously, Scarlett.

SCARLETT   You think I'm kiddin? You think I sit around and
watch game shows and uh stare out the window
waitin for the next volunteer? No way, girlie, I git
it ONNN.

CHRISTINE   You're. . . sexually active, then?

SCARLETT   Shocked, aren't you, pretty pea?

CHRISTINE   No.

SCARLETT   YOU ARE TOO, YOU LYING BITCH!!

CHRISTINE   All right, I will admit, I am. . . surprised. I suppose
the public perception of handicapped people is
somewhat skewered.

SCARLETT   You think you're bettern me, dontcha?

CHRISTINE   Oh, Scarlett, really I. . .

SCARLETT   Well I'll tell you somethin, Christine, my boyfriend wouldn't rub your tittie. And you think he's
handicapped? No way, babe, I'm not fucking a
freak.

CHRISTINE   Well, I'm very happy for you, really, Scarlett.

SCARLETT   Bullshit, you think it's sick.

CHRISTINE   No, honestly, Scarlett, I don't! I think everybody
            deserves to have a happy sex life.

SCARLETT   Yeah? Wanna hear more?

CHRISTINE   Sure!

SCARLETT   But don't print this part in your article, right, just
            the crap about how noble I am copin on my own
            and that shit, and how good the United Church
            is helpin me out, all that shit, right?

CHRISTINE   Scarlett, I won't print anything that you don't
            want me to. I despise journalists that do that kind
            of thing. I want you to think of me as a friend.
            Maybe we could even go out sometime, catch a
            movie, or go to dinner. . .

SCARLETT   Sure, if you like.

CHRISTINE   So! How did it all start with your boyfriend?

SCARLETT   It all started one night. I'd just been watching TV
            for sixteen hours straight, from eight in the morn-
            ing, right? And that's hard on the eyes; I was bone
            tired. So I go to bed. I look out the window and
            there's no moon, right? And I lie there for hours,
            can't sleep, itchy, bored, just wishin I was dead,
            as usual, when I hear my door open.

CHRISTINE   Were you frightened?

SCARLETT   I couldnta cared. I thought it was, you know, a
            guy with a knife, come to carve me up. I thought
            good, great, what a way to go. I laughed thinkin a
            Monica—she's my morning volunteer—thinkin a
            her comin in findin me dead—so I wait to be cut,
            but I don't hear nothin, nothin. I figure he's in
            his socks, not a sound then. . . he sits on the edge
            of my bed, and and and, and then he start. . . he
            start. . . he start. . . touchin my foot, just touchin
            my foot so soft, and nice, and I. . . laugh. I laugh
            and laugh, and, Christine, I don't think I ever
            laughed so long and so long in my life.

CHRISTINE   Who was it?

SCARLETT   That's the question, isn't it, Chris? Who the hell
            is it?

CHRISTINE   Did he. . . ever come again?

SCARLETT   He come every time there isn't no moon; in like
            a big cat, sit on the bed, and me, like a big piece
            of fruit. . .

            Dance music starts. SCARLETT gets up.

            . . . explodin in the heat, exploding up and out the
            whole night. I can MOVE when my boy comes.

She twirls.

I am movin; I know I am. I am turnin and swishin
and holdin. . .

> *A MAN enters. He and SCARLETT dance roman-
> tically around the set. He leaves her back in
> her chair, immobile, and exits.*

. . . like eels. You ever seen eels? Lamprey eels,
brilliant light moving fast fast, they swim from the
Saint John River down to Montego Bay to spurt
their young. I swim like that, coloured-up, bright
and fast when my boy comes, swirlin and movin
in the dark, no moon. . .

CHRISTINE   Hey, is he handsome?

SCARLETT   I tole you there's no moon.

CHRISTINE   You mean you haven't—

SCARLETT   He's my midnight man, you dick! My midnight
man; he is my midnight man, get it? You can't
SEE night; you can't SEE when there's no moon.
Why? Why do you think it's so big to see your
boyfriend—two eyes, nose, a mouth, what the diff,
what the hell is the—

CHRISTINE   I must go; I. . . have an appointment.

SCARLETT   You're not gonna print that.

CHRISTINE   I have a job, Scarlett, I have a child to support. . .

SCARLETT   I'll slit your throat if ya print that.

CHRISTINE   Goodbye.

       SCARLETT grabs CHRISTINE's clothing.

SCARLETT   PLEASE!! PLEASE!! Please, Christine, my old lady
            and old man, they're old, my mum's had a stroke,
            my dad's got MS, this'd kill 'em, please!!

CHRISTINE   That is not my business, Scarlett. Scarlett, let go
            of me—LET GO!

SCARLETT   Reverend Pete and everybody down the church,
            they'd think I was a slut, they'd send me to the
            freak house.

       They struggle.

CHRISTINE   Let me go!!

       SCARLETT falls on top of CHRISTINE.

SCARLETT   You're gonna kill me, you're gonna kill me.

       CHRISTINE rolls her off and onto the floor.

CHRISTINE   You are trying to obstruct the freedom of the press, lady.

SCARLETT   You can't do this, you can't do this!

CHRISTINE   *(frees herself and gets away)* I'm sorry. I'm doing it.

SCARLETT   I'll see you in hell!!

This stops CHRISTINE.

CHRISTINE   What?

SCARLETT   I said you'll go right to hell for this!!

CHRISTINE   I don't believe in hell.

SCARLETT   Joke's on you, girl, 'cause I'm in it, right now, live from hell, and if you do this, you're gonna be burning here with me. Maybe not today, maybe not tomorrow, but soon, soon, you'll be whizzing down the highway with a large group of handsome friends to some ski resort or other, and your male driver will decide to pass on the right. You will turn over and over, knocking into each other's skulls, breaking each other's necks like eggs in a bag, falling through windshields; it's gonna rain blood and I will open my big jaws and swallow youuuu! YOU will spend the rest of eternity inside me. Inside my. . . body and ooooh time goes slowwwww. . .

CHRISTINE   You're crazy.

SCARLETT   I am waiting for you, Chrissy, I'm waiting for you, Chrissy, I am waiting for you, Chrissy, I am. . .

CHRISTINE   STOP THAT. Stop that craziness NOW. There is no such thing, there is no such thing as any of that, ANY of it. You live and you die in your own body and you go up to or just nowhere.

SCARLETT   Into the middle of Scarlett. . .

CHRISTINE   You don't know ANYTHING.

SCARLETT   Inside my big wet behind. . .

CHRISTINE   Stop it. Stop saying those things.

SCARLETT   In the bummy of a big dead fish. . .

CHRISTINE   Stop it. I said stop it now.

SCARLETT   Your left arm and your head too, Chrissy, gonna be severed. You'll be all over the highway and your mean little soul will. . .

          CHRISTINE *beats* SCARLETT *to the ground, screaming.*

CHRISTINE   STOP IT! STOP IT! *(kicking her)* STOP IT! STOP IT!

CHRISTINE collapses.

SCARLETT breathes with difficulty.

Oh no. Oh no. Scarlett, are you okay? You're okay. You're okay. Your mother will be by soon, or a volunteer, and, and I'll call, I I I'll call an ambulance. You shouldn't have made me do that, Scarlett. You shouldn't have made me kick you like that. The way you you you talked to me like that. Like like like you belong. In the world. As if you belong. Where did you get that feeling? I want it. I need it.

Pause. She's about to exit.

I need it.

SCARLETT   OOOOOOH! Come down and kiss me, put your tongue in my mouth!! Come on, NOW, RIGHT now, there's no one around, right now, on the ground, do me, kiss me, come down and kiss me, like a lion, so hot right here, right now, swirl, swirl me twirl, twirl me, make me light, light exploding into. . . *(laughs)*

> *CHRISTINE returns, swooping down like a condor, and gives SCARLETT the kiss of death. SCARLETT, thinking it is her lover, responds passionately and then, without air, dies.*

ISOBEL   *(to* CHRISTINE, *touching her)* SLAVE! You are a slave
of the Lion! You lie with him, you laugh, you let
him bite your neck, you spread your legs. You will
take me to him now.

> *Music, blackout. Lights up on* CHRISTINE's
> *office. She is moving things in an angry way.*

Shhh. I wait for the Lion!!

> RODNEY, *a middle-aged man with a stoop,*
> CHRISTINE's *research assistant, comes in and*
> *waits until she addresses him. He has an arm-*
> *load of papers.*

CHRISTINE   Yes, Rodney, what is it?

RODNEY   I've. . . uh. . . brought the research material you
asked for.

CHRISTINE   Good. Great. Thank you. . . how was your
weekend?

RODNEY   Quiet.

CHRISTINE   Rodney. Rodney—Rodney, I told you I wanted
stats on MS, multiple sclerosis, not just "handicapped people." I wanted information on MS!

RODNEY   You did NOT specify multiple sclerosis, Christine.

CHRISTINE   Oh yes I most certainly did, I said—

RODNEY   I have it on tape, Christine!

CHRISTINE   Rodney! Are you or are you not a professional researcher?

RODNEY   Yes.

CHRISTINE   Well then start doing professional work! NOW! Or you are out. Is that understood? IS THAT UNDERSTOOD?

RODNEY   . . . of. . . course. . .

CHRISTINE exits. RODNEY is at his desk.

You will NOT EVER SPEAK TO ME THAT WAY AGAIN, CHRISTINE. YOU WILL NOT TREAT ME AS AN OBJECT, DO YOU UNDERSTAND? Is that understood? IS THAT UNDERSTOOD??

A knock on the door.

Yes? Hello. May I help you?

MICHAEL   Yes, I'm looking for a Rodney LeHavre—I was directed to this office.

RODNEY   I. . . am. . . Mr. LeHavre.

MICHAEL   Rodney?

RODNEY   Do I know you?

MICHAEL   Michael. . . Lind. . . from St. George's, '60 to '64.
          How are you? You remember me, don't you?

RODNEY   Michael. . . Lind? No. No, I'm afraid I don't, I'm
          sorry. Were you in my class?

MICHAEL   Yeah, yeah, we were good friends for a while even;
          don't you remember? Come on. We played chess.
          You were a great player. You taught me. . . how to
          play. You must remember.

RODNEY   Chess.

MICHAEL   I guess you don't remember. I'm sorry. I was sure
          that you'd remember. I. . . I. . . *(backing out)*

RODNEY   Would you like to come in and sit down? I can
          take ten minutes, I think. Would you like to
          sit down?

MICHAEL   Oh, oh, okay, if you don't mind. . .

RODNEY   No. A cup of coffee. . . I could—get the secretary
          Sherry—to—

MICHAEL   *(laughs)* You've got to remember the fly collection.
          It was really hot. July, I think. We caught it must

have been fifty houseflies, and, and we stuck them with Elmer's glue, to a piece of bristol board. To a big piece of bristol board. And labelled them in Latin. Don't you remember? You must remember.

RODNEY   Wait a minute. . . wait a minute. . . yeah, yeah, and we even named them, didn't we? Didn't we name each one?

MICHAEL ·   Yeah, yeah. . . I'll never forget. You even named one Clarence. I thought it was brilliant.

RODNEY   Right! And yours were all names like Fred, Joe, Cindy, weren't they? Right!

MICHAEL   And yours were all royalty—Elizabeth, Margaret, Clarence. God!

RODNEY   God. A fly collection. So what did we *do* with it?

MICHAEL   I think. . . we had it arranged. . . to show someone. A colleague of my father's. Someone in insect. . .

RODNEY   Entomology.

MICHAEL   Yeah, that's it. And it was raining or something. . .

RODNEY   Pouring, yes, pouring, and all the flies—

RODNEY &
MICHAEL   —FELL OFF THE BRISTOL BOARD!

RODNEY   God. Michael Lind. Michael LIND! I'm sorry.

CHRISTINE *(off)* Rodney, I need that material as SOON as possible, please!

MICHAEL   Well I see that you have to get back to work; I'd better go. . . ahhh. . . just before I go, there's one thing. I uh. . . this is going to sound strange, but. . . I've been having. . . sort of. . . dreams. . . about. . . back then. I. . . have them a lot—

RODNEY   Oh?

MICHAEL   Yes, only. . . I always wake up at the same spot, fairly distressed, actually, and. . . I just. . . wondered. . . if you could. . . help me. . . remember. . . what actually happened. Back then. . . when we were. . . kids. Do you think you could—

RODNEY   Sure, I could try. . .

MICHAEL   Okay, let's start at the beginning. It was something to do with chess.

RODNEY   Chess.

MICHAEL   You loved to play chess. You. . . brought me to your house after school. It was a Tuesday, I think, cold. We went through a shortcut, it said "Pedestrians Only." I thought it said "Protestants Only," and I was terrified.

RODNEY laughs.

And we went to your room, with all the paper
airplanes hanging from the ceiling all over the
room! And we lay on the floor. Do you remember?
You remember lying on the floor? Rodney, your
carpet. Your carpet was brown and orange, sort
of circles or something. There was the sound of
a snow blower outside. My queen. You took my
queen. And then, and then, Rodney, didn't we
laugh, or or or or. . . some touch, some touch,
Rodney, and you made a strange sound. What
was that sound? Please help me! I need to go back
there. I need to go back there, you see? You were
the only—friend that I—we saw the world the
same way. Remember? We saw the world the same
way. I want to go back there. *(caresses RODNEY's
shoulder)* I want to go back there. . .

RODNEY   I want to go back there, too. I want to go back
there, too.

*MICHAEL and RODNEY embrace. RODNEY makes
the sound. MICHAEL pushes him back and
throws him to the ground.*

MICHAEL   QUEER!! Queer queer queer queer queer queer
QUEER! FAIRY SISSY LITTLE CREEP!! DON'T YOU
EVER ever remember again. YOU have WRECKED
my life—your slimy memory, using me over and
over and over again like an old porno magazine.

You will RELINQUISH that memory, you will wipe it OUT, YOU understand?

RODNEY   You're crazy; you need psychiatric. . .

MICHAEL   You will NOT remember me again because if you do, if you do, I will feel it, oh yes, and I will come and I will kill you. I could feel you remembering, almost daily. I would be in the middle, the middle of a crucial business meeting all the way in Vancouver and suddenly I would feel you. . . holding my memory, turning it over and over, folding it, caressing it, reliving it, SPEWING, spewing your filth all over me. How how I always wondered. How could you do it in the middle of the day? Did you do it here, at work, at this desk? Is this where you—

RODNEY   Anywhere I can, Michael. You see, my life has been terribly disappointing.

MICHAEL   You will. . . free me—

RODNEY   Of course. I'll try, but memory. . . does seem to have a will of its own. I can't really help what—

> MICHAEL *hits him. They fight, rolling and punching, and end up on the floor. Very, very slowly* MICHAEL *raises his head and extends his tongue.* RODNEY *does the same. They come together and their tongues touch. It is*

an ecstatic moment for both of them. MICHAEL
pulls out a knife. RODNEY *takes it from him and
cuts his throat.* MICHAEL *dies. Music. The actor
playing* MICHAEL *gets up and exits.* ISOBEL *goes
to* RODNEY *and touches him, then* RODNEY *gets
up and straightens himself.*

RODNEY   "Hello, welcome to St. George's. My name is
Rodney LeHavre, grade seven, and you're. . . ?
Michael Lind! Welcome! You just came
from Vancouver? I have a cousin there! Do
you play chess?" Chess, every day. . . chess,
Monday, Tuesday, Wednesday, Thursday, chess,
with. . . Michael. . . at school, at my house, at his
house, in his room, lying on our stomachs star-
ing at the chess board. He sticks his tongue out
at me because he had just captured my queen
and then I stuck my tongue out back at him and
he moved forward just a bit till his tongue was
touching mine, and my whole life jumped into
my tongue. We didn't move, just lay there touching tongues. "Would you boys like some tuna
sandwiches?" His mother, the best mother in the
world, with her red bangles and bourbon sour
at six. "Okay, Mrs. Lind, thanks!" And we had a
secret, an atomic secret nobody else in the whole
entire world knew, that we had touched tongues,
oh OH; wrote his name, MICHAEL, over and over
one thousand times, one thousand times; on the
fifth day, the fifth day after, I'm at the blackboard
doing math, very good at math, superb mind for

mathematics—the other boys jealous, always been jealous of my superior brain, throwing spitballs, used to that, yelling "froggy, froggy frog" because of my francophone name, used to that—I turn, I catch his face white darkened so quickly like a sky; he caught, he knew, suddenly he knew, Michael, that he had been playing chess with the loser "FROGGY, HEY FROGGY." They scream "HEY FROG." He stands up! They look expectantly, is the new kid going to defend his friend? What's he going to say? I think to myself, "Oh thank you, Michael, thank you, thank you. The first to ever defend me, oh what what are you going to say to defend me?" He takes a breath, I'm holding mine, he smiles, he speaks, he says: "Is he a frog. . . OR A TOAD!!" They laugh and laugh and laugh, screaming their laughter, slapping their desks, shaking their fists, triumphing a new member of the PACK!! Is he a frog, or a toad— Am I a frog or am I a toad?

SHERRY enters.

SHERRY   RODDEE! RODDEEE!! Baby bunny.

ISOBEL   She!

SHERRY   You'll never guess what I have! Milk chocolate bar with lots of gushy cream in it. Two squares for you, and two squares for me.

ISOBEL   She!

SHERRY   One hundred and forty calories a square, who
              gives a shit. I heard Christine chewin ya out.
              What a fuckin cow.

ISOBEL   She. . . I see, I smell the spray, the Lion's spray. . .

SHERRY   *(notices that RODNEY is very upset)* What happened?

              > SHERRY *runs from* RODNEY's *office back home
              > to the apartment she shares with her boy-
              > friend of two years,* EDWARD, *an out-of-work
              > actor. When she comes in he is practising a
              > tap routine for an audition. Newspapers are
              > all over the floor.*

              Jesus I'm peed off—I'm standing on the escalator,
              right? Goin down to the subway? My back hurts,
              I don't feel like takin the stairs? So I'm standin
              there when this woman shoves by me right into
              the wall and goes, "Can't *you* move? Some people
              are in a hurry!" And I just STAND there like a fuck-
              ing WETWIPE with my mouth open. FUCK if I see
              that bitch again—

EDWARD   That's very interesting, Sherry.

SHERRY   Whatcha workin on? That dance tryout thing?

EDWARD   Uh, no. I'm fixing the faulty wiring with my feet;
              it's magic, Sherry, really! Right through the—

SHERRY	Ah jeez, you're not mad at me again, are ya? Whad I do now?
EDWARD	I don't know, Sherry, what did you do now?
SHERRY	I get off work at five thirty, Ed, it's ten to six. What the hell am I supposed to do? Fly home?
EDWARD	I phoned work at four o'clock, Sherry, and Arlene said that you had left for the day.
SHERRY	Oh, well THAT—I was havin a coffee and a piece of cake with Rodney, he—
EDWARD	Don't lie, please.
SHERRY	I was, Eddie, ask Rodney, ask—
EDWARD	You've rehearsed them all.
SHERRY	Listen to me! Rodney had some kind of fit today. Christine just about called the cops, he was yelling and screaming at nobody all afternoon—he's right nuts.
EDWARD	It is a skilful liar, it is.
SHERRY	*Don't call me "it."*
EDWARD	I beg your pardon?

SHERRY	Have you been drinking? Or doin coke or some shit? You have, haven't you? You—
EDWARD	We're out of toilet paper.
SHERRY	No, there's more right under the—
EDWARD	No there's NOT!
SHERRY	All right, I'll go and get some now—
EDWARD	YOU'LL stay right where you are, Sherry.
SHERRY	Fuck you!
EDWARD	Please. PLEASE, I'm asking you. Don't leave me alone—here—I don't want to be alone.
SHERRY	Aww, Eddie, you know I love you, don't you.
EDWARD	If—if you're not happy with my performance in bed. . . I wish you'd just. . . tell me and—and—
SHERRY	Honey, I love your performance in bed.
EDWARD	You don't really, do you?
SHERRY	Listen, I was just tellin Arlene today you got the best hands of I bet any guy there is on the whole fuckin planet!

EDWARD   You were?

SHERRY   The way you touch me, Eddie, Christ, I feel like
           a whole bouquet, you know? A bouquet of red
           flowers just. . . poppin open, pop pop pop pop
           pop, just like on one of them nature specials. I
           love makin love with you. I think about it all day.

EDWARD   *(kissing her)* Oh! Oh! I've been thinking about
           you too, all day, every day.

SHERRY   Oh, Eddie, I want you.

EDWARD   You want me. . . ? Fuck you!

SHERRY   Did you not get that part in the TV series?
           About the runaway kid or whatever? Is that why
           you're—Eddie, what's wrong? Did I say some-
           thing wrong?

EDWARD   YOU ARE A FLAMING ASSHOLE!

SHERRY   Eddie!

EDWARD   Who are you dreaming about every night?

SHERRY   What?

EDWARD   Every night you're moaning like an animal in
           heat—who?

SHERRY   What?

EDWARD   Who are you dreaming about, Sherry?

SHERRY   Nobody! I'm not dreaming about—nobody.

EDWARD   WHO ARE YOU DREAMING ABOUT?

SHERRY   Just forget it. I'm going over to Arlene's; I'll see
              you later.

EDWARD   You tell me who you are dreaming about or I will
              cancel the wedding.

SHERRY   Eddie.

EDWARD   I will. . . TODAY, if you don't stop lying to me,
              treating me like a fucking maggot—

SHERRY   I'm not lying to you, Ed, please, just—

EDWARD   I'll cancel the wedding! I'll phone up Father
              Hayes.

SHERRY   I paid five thousand dollars for that dress, Eddie.

EDWARD   I don't give a flying fuck what you paid for it.

SHERRY   EDDIE, my mum's got her ticket from Florida, my
              sisters—

EDWARD   *(on the phone)* I'd like to speak to Father Hayes, please—

SHERRY   OKAY OKAY OKAY OKAY, you're right, you're right. There is someone I'm dreaming about; it's. . . uh. . .

EDWARD   It's him, isn't it?

SHERRY   Him? Who? *(makes the connection)* Eddie, THAT is not fair!

EDWARD   It's him, isn't it?

SHERRY   I think I'm going to be sick!

EDWARD   That was the best you ever had, wasn't it? It was the only fuck you ever respected, wasn't it? WASN'T IT, SHERRY?

                  SHERRY cries.

              WASN'T IT? WASN'T IT?

SHERRY   NO!

EDWARD   Listen to me. You don't tell me the truth right now I'll cancel the wedding. RIGHT now, I'll call up Father Hayes and I'll cancel the whole thing for good.

SHERRY   Eddie, please!

                He pulls out his phone again and begins to
                search for the number.

EDWARD   St. Paul's Cathedral, St. Paul's—532—

                SHERRY reaches for the phone, distressed, but
                EDWARD keeps it out of her reach but slides it
                back into his pocket when she says:

SHERRY   Okay! Okay okay okay!

EDWARD   You admit?

                SHERRY nods.

SHERRY   That. . .

                EDWARD moves to pull out his phone again.

                That he's the best fuck I ever had.

EDWARD   Now we are cookin with GAS. This is what I
                always knew in my heart, never DARED with all
                this MeToo shit going down. Come on, come on,
                tell me if I'm going to be your husband. I want to
                know it all.

SHERRY   But what should I—

EDWARD   The truth!! I know how hard it is for you after a
          lifetime of female. . . conniving and guile, but
          let's do it! Come on! Tell me, tell me how you
          led him on.

SHERRY   Led. . . him. . . on??

EDWARD   HOW YOU LAID YOUR TRAP! Come on, what was it
          you were wearing? Wasn't it that. . . pink. . . what
          is it called? Sherry, what is it called?

          SHERRY *is saying what she thinks he wants
          to hear because she is scared, but it is like
          excrement in her mouth, and* EDWARD *is both
          gratified and ripped apart at the same time
          by what he hears.*

SHERRY   Pink. . . thong?

EDWARD   That's it! And what else, what else?

SHERRY   Ahhh. . .

EDWARD   Come on!

SHERRY   No—bra?

EDWARD   Yes? YES!

SHERRY   I was a real—tease with the guy?

EDWARD   Good, good, Sherry, the truth is good.
           And. . . AND. . . You were walking home from the
           subway, yes?

SHERRY   Yes.

EDWARD   About one thirty in the morning, yes?

SHERRY   Yes. Well. I had been at my great aunt's doin—

EDWARD   I don't give a fuck where you were, Sherry, you
           were walking home, one thirty in the morning,
           right?

SHERRY   Right.

EDWARD   And you hear steps behind you.

SHERRY   Steps.

EDWARD   Clack clack clack like cowboy boots.

SHERRY   Clack. Clack.

EDWARD   And a voice. . .

SHERRY   Like a housefly.

EDWARD   A VOICE.

SHERRY   Asks me if I had been seein that. . . porno show
           down the street.

EDWARD   And you said. . .

SHERRY   I didn't say, Ed, I walked faster.

EDWARD   But your heels, were so high, so provocative, that
           you turned on your ankle.

SHERRY   I sprained my ankle.

EDWARD   And he grabbed you.

SHERRY   By the arm!

EDWARD   He was all man.

SHERRY   Oh no! No! And. . . and. . . he throws me between
           two houses, on the cement, near the trash.

EDWARD   Where were all the people, Sherry?

SHERRY   I guess they thought we were married, they
           thought it was okay.

EDWARD   You were very aroused.

SHERRY   *(very obviously was not)* No. . .

EDWARD   And he—pushed you back to the cement?

SHERRY   When I tried to get up.

EDWARD   And? And?

SHERRY   He starts. . . smashin my head against the cement!

EDWARD   You're so frightened, breathing fast, like an animal!

SHERRY   He—he—he kept telling me that he was going to
                kill me.

EDWARD   And you're very aroused!

SHERRY   He—he—

EDWARD   You're moaning with ecstasy.

SHERRY   "I'm gonna kill you, bitch," he kept sayin, "I'm
                gonna kill you, bitch."

EDWARD   The hottest sex you ever had!

SHERRY   And. . . and. . . I lie there for hours, passed out,
                half listening to the cars drivin by, half letting the
                gravel cut into my face. I laid there for hours!

EDWARD   But happy, right? You finally got it GOOD.

SHERRY   Until the lady's puttin out her garbage!

EDWARD	You told her, of course, that you are the snake. Because the snake tempts others to sin, uh-huh? SATAN tempts others to sin. Say it, Sherry. Come on, "I am the snake," come on, "I am the snake," "I am the snake," come on COME ON.
SHERRY	I. . . am. . . the snake.
EDWARD	With the diamond back, glittering.
SHERRY	Yeah. I am. The snake. With the back.
EDWARD	Oh yes!! You ARE the snake, baby, come on, "I am the snake!"
SHERRY	I am. The snake! I am the snake! I am the snake! I AM THE SNAKE I AM THE SNAKE I AM THE SNAKE I AM THE SNAAAAAAAAKE!

> SHERRY *breaks down in tears. She collapses on the floor.* EDWARD *cleans up and then sits down.*

Eddie? Will you come with me tomorrow then to Ashley's to pick out a pattern? Like I've made the appointment and everything, Ed, and after all, you are going to have to live with the dishes. I mean, I know guys hate goin in there, all guys do, but everyone that gets married goes to Ashley's, everyone that gets married—

EDWARD   All right. But nothing with flowers on it. I just
           want something clean, maybe—white, with a
           black stripe.

           She thinks, changes her mind, then turns away.

           ISOBEL *enters the room and offers her hand to*
           SHERRY, *who takes it, gratefully. Arm in arm,*
           they walk away from SHERRY *and* EDWARD's
           apartment to a graveyard. At first ISOBEL *is*
           helping SHERRY, *but by the time they reach*
           the graveyard, it is SHERRY *who helps* ISOBEL
           find her grave, and gently lays her down, and
           disappears.

           In the graveyard, sitting on another tombstone,
           is BEN, *the man who killed* ISOBEL *seventeen*
           years before, and JOAN.

           A group of mourners exit, leaving BEN *and his*
           mother alone.

JOAN   Dear, you're looking quite uncomfortable, shall
           we go?

BEN   Yeah, yeah, let's go. No. No. Let's stay here.
           Here, sit on a tombstone, why dontcha? *(read-*
           ing) "Harvey J. Walker, 1920–1973." What's that
           make him?

JOAN   Dear, it's getting quite chilly, don't you think?

BEN	It's summer, Joanie!
JOAN	Yes, dear, but there is a wind! I'm afraid my silly old hair will just—
BEN	JOAN! I wanna siddown and pay my respects. SID-DOWN! SIT DOWN!
JOAN	(*sitting down awkwardly*) All right. Somebody hasn't watered these impatiens in a very long time. Poor old Father Hayes; I will miss him.
BEN	He was an old fruit.
JOAN	Benny, he was not, how can you say that about Father Hayes?
BEN	Because he talked like a fruit; he walked like one too.
JOAN	Now now, you don't mean that.
BEN	I sure as hell do.
JOAN	BEN, PLEASE, your language!!
BEN	So, whaddya been up to, Joan? Lots a charity work? What?
JOAN	Yes, I'm still working in the shop, at the hospital.

BEN	What about bridge, you still play bridge?
JOAN	Oh yes, every week. Heavens, I guess it's been every week for the last. . . fifteen years. Ben, I wish you would call me Mum.
BEN	I can't. I told you that before.
JOAN	You are my son. We've had you since you were three weeks old, for heaven's sake.
BEN	I don't give a shit. You're Joan. I like you; you're just not my mother.
JOAN	You break my heart. Christine still calls me Mum.
BEN	Christine's different.
JOAN	How? How is Christine different?
BEN	'Cause. . . she's. . . like you, see; she's the same. Her mother was some kinda student or something, her father a professor or some shit, me, I wasn't from nothin. I'm different, I'm different from you, see?
JOAN	I love you, Ben, I hope you. . .
BEN	Don't say that word.
JOAN	I'm sorry, but it's true. I love every hair on your sweet head. . .

BEN	Joan.
JOAN	And I will till the day I die.
BEN	DO YOU LOVE ME?
JOAN	Well yes, I just—
BEN	Do you love me?
JOAN	Terribly.
BEN	Well then gimme some money.
JOAN	I beg your pardon?
BEN	I need a loan. About sixty thousand bucks. And I need it tonight.
JOAN	Oh so that's why you agreed to come with me to Father Hayes's funeral. Stupid me, I actually thought. . .
BEN	Shutup. I came because I knew it meant something to you; I hadn't seen you in a while—
JOAN	Eight months.
BEN	Yeah, well, I was busy.
JOAN	You're only seeing me because you want money.

BEN	Shutup, don't give me that shit. . .
JOAN	It's obviously true, Ben.
BEN	Okay, it's true. Can you get the money?
JOAN	What do you need it for?
BEN	I said can you get it?
JOAN	I don't know, Ben. I don't know until you tell me what you need it for.
BEN	Okay, I'm leaving.
JOAN	Ben WAIT, WAIT. *(crying)* I'm sorry.
BEN	WELL don't cry. I hate it when an old woman cries, it's friggin gross; youse are ugly enough to begin with but when you start with the water. . .
JOAN	Ben, that's enough.
BEN	I'm just being straight, Joan. Come on, the old "visage" is NOT what it used to be. HEY, you can take a little tease, can't ya?
JOAN	Well I know I've aged, dear, but I didn't think—
BEN	You're old and ugly. But you're okay. Want a smoke?

JOAN	No thank you, Ben, you know I don't.
BEN	The cancer thing, right, right, well I don't give a shit, myself, so I'm gonna smoke myself sick.
JOAN	Ben, why do you say you don't care?
BEN	'Cause I'm a sittin duck. Unless you give me that cash money now, I'll be dead news anyways, so what do I care.
JOAN	I don't follow you, Ben.
BEN	I'm saying that there's people after me, Joanie, bad bad dudes. These jokers don't think nothin, nothin of blowin a guy's head off and stickin him in a trunk.
JOAN	Oh, Benny, how did you get involved with these. . .
BEN	Don't ask questions, Joanie, for crying out loud. I did time in a federal penitentiary. I did twenty years in friggin Collins Bay; the place is crawlin with creeps; they follow you out. . .
JOAN	Why are they. . . after you?
BEN	Why are they after me? Why are they after me? You are askin me why they are after me? Why do you think?

JOAN	Well goodness, anybody who knows anything knows you did not kill that little girl. All the magazines wrote about the suppressed evidence, and impossibility of the time factor, everybody knows it was a miscarriage of justice—
BEN	I know that you know that, butcha think the turkeys know that? Hey, they just gotta feel upper than somebody, right? They're the lowest on the social ladder, they gotta have somebody lower, that's me, scum of the earth.
JOAN	Oh, Benny.
BEN	You never thought I done it.
JOAN	Not for a second.
BEN	May I ask why?
JOAN	Because—because—you would fall asleep only in my arms till you were six years old.
BEN	ONLY IN YOUR ARMS.
JOAN	And you brushed my hair; your favourite pastime in the world was for us to lie on the bed and you would brush and brush my hair. My hair was long then, black. . .
BEN	I still like brushin chicks' hair.

JOAN   I always knew. I always knew it wasn't you.

BEN   I know. I know you always knew that.

JOAN   I am your mother. . .

BEN   NO!

JOAN   I AM.

BEN   You are not! You are. . . my guardian, LIKE a
            mother to me, not my mother. My mother is prob-
            ably some whore living outta Loblaws bags now.

JOAN   Oh, Benny.

BEN   Are you gonna give me the cash?

JOAN   Just. . . please, please tell me what it's for? Please,
            darling?

BEN   Surgery. Changin my face so those jokers won't
            know me, then I'm gonna start in on the pasta,
            the milkshakes, gain fifty pounds, then dye the
            hair red.

JOAN   But surely that won't cost—

BEN   LET ME FINISH. Christ, did ya ever let anybody
            finish anything?

JOAN   I'm sorry.

BEN   You better be. Now where was I. . .

JOAN   About why you need so much—

BEN   Okay, after the looks change, I go into business.
       I got an idea for a business, gonna make me a
       millionaire. Alls I gotta do is have some cash up
       front.

JOAN   Ben, dear, I don't mean to be discouraging, but
       I've watched so many of these schemes of yours—

BEN   What?

JOAN   Fail!!

BEN   They didn't fail! They didn't fail, they just didn't
       work 'cause of people rippin me off, 'cause my
       heart was too big!! Well this time I learned my
       lesson. I know, I know to be ruthless, okay?

JOAN   Well I don't think you have to be "ruthless." I
       mean Walter was a brilliant businessman, but he
       was never never—

BEN   (spits) HE WAS A SON OF A BITCH.

JOAN   Walter loved you, Benny.

BEN	Don't you mention that man's name; the man was a pig.
JOAN	Ben, you are talking about your father, my husband.
BEN	NOT MY FATHER NOT MY FATHER. YOU only saw one face, Joanie, one WALTER face, the other face was secret, between him and me, only I saw the. . .
JOAN	Oh, Ben, how can you—
BEN	He he he he he used to force me. . .
JOAN	He forced you to do what?
BEN	Well. . . forget it.
JOAN	Ben, please, I don't understand what you—
BEN	WHY DO YOU THINK THIS BOY IS HELL? I was hell for you from the time I was seven, killin the cats, wrecking the car, sellin your stereo. WHY? 'Cause my mother was a fifteen-year-old kid from Gerrard and Parliament with stringy hair. . . who couldn't say her alphabet? You think it's that? Why do you think it is, Joanie? Why do you think I am hell?
JOAN	I think that when we told you that you were adopted, you were crushed and we were never able to help you.

BEN	No. So whaddya think it is, Joan?
JOAN	. . . Something. . . Walter. . . ?
BEN	Yeah. Yeah. Yeah. . . something Walter did.
JOAN	You are saying that he. . . did something to you— he struck you?
BEN	Joanie, bein hit, I wouldnta minded; hell it was a relief when it was that. It's. . . the other. . .
JOAN	It's not true.
BEN	You never noticed anything? NOTHIN strange? Whydja think, whydja think he left the bed every night?
JOAN	To have a snack; he. . . always said that he had had a. . . snack.
BEN	(laughs) Yeah right.
JOAN	I'm. . . really in a state of shock.
BEN	Believe me, Joan.
JOAN	I thought I knew Walter so well. . .
BEN	Yeah.

JOAN	OH GOD. My little boy, my poor little. . .
BEN	Poor Joanie, no one told her. No one ever told her that ninety-five percent of the human population is maggots. You got fooled into thinkin life was nice tea parties and hot cocoa after skatin and tuckin your kids in and singing a pretty song about the fuckin moon. . . 'Member that rabbit I used to have?
JOAN	Honey.
BEN	Yeah, Honey. Well, Honey always made me think of you, you know, with those big wide-apart eyes, believe everything, thinkin everything is nice, so trusting. She was so trustin it made me mad, you know? Like why do you trust me? Don't you know I could pull your eyes out? You should hop away when my hands are in your cage, hop away, you stupid pest, don't just stand there. With those eyes.
JOAN	Is that why you—
BEN	I DON'T LIKE STUPIDITY.
JOAN	Oh dear.
BEN	Look, Joan, I'm short on time here, so do we have a deal?

JOAN	Sixty. . . thousand. . . ?
BEN	You got it.
JOAN	Oh Ben. Oh Ben. Walter. I am shattered to know that my Walter—
BEN	Hey. Would I lie to you, Joanie? Just to score some cash? Come on. . .
JOAN	Now I know, Ben, I know. . .
BEN	Whaddya know?
JOAN	Her picture, in the papers, on all those posters, that picture, her eyes, she had unusually trusting, wide-apart—
BEN	Back off, I'm tellin ya, Joanie—
JOAN	YOU HATE TRUSTING EYES because—they reminded you of me and how. . . I trusted Walter, how I let it go on, how dumb I was, how dumb I was; you were killing me, killing—WALTER! It's all my fault!! That little girl's death is all my fault!
BEN	There's one thing, you know. There's one thing that I always. . . wanted to tell somebody and that is that. . . I done her a favour. I was—kindly— yeah. See, I pull her outta the car and throw her

on the cement in front of the warehouse there, and. . . I put my hands around her neck and she says to me, she says, "Please," she says, "Please no strangle, I so. . . scared of strangle" in this. . . voice of breath, just. . . purely of breath, and I stopped, eh? I stepped out of the twister, 'cause that's what it's like, Joanie, when you're doin somethin like that, you're inside a twister and to step out is like. . . liftin two hundred pounds, but I did 'cause she touched me, okay? She touched me, right—she was me, right? She was me, under Walter, asking him, askin him "Please, Daddy, please, please, Daddy," so I done what I always wanted Walter to do, what I always wished—what I wished every night.

JOAN backs away in horror. ISOBEL approaches with her weapon.

ISOBEL   BEN. . . ja. . . men.

He looks.

BEN ja men BEN ja men.

BEN   Who are you?

ISOBEL   Is. . . o. . . bel.

BEN   Isobel.

ISOBEL	July. Isobel in July—July the one, remember? Don't you remember? CANADA Day, day for CANADA birthday. I selling tickets, tickets on a Chrysler car, for boys and girls club, one dollar fifty for a ticket. I have five tickets left. Don't you remember? I see you in park. It is raining. In my park I ask you, "You want to buy ticket on a Chrysler car?" You say "Yes, yes, I buy all five. All five tickets. Come into my car, come into my silver car with dark red seats, come into my car. I will give you the money for the tickets; I have the money in my car," you said. . .
BEN	I'm hallucinatin.
ISOBEL	I'm Isobel.
BEN	You're a picture.
ISOBEL	I'm Isobel.
BEN	What. . . do you want?
ISOBEL	I have come.
BEN	What do you want?
ISOBEL	I am here.
BEN	WELL GO AWAY! You hear me? GO AWAY.

> *She is about to kill him with the stick—the forces of vengeance and forgiveness warring inside her. Forgiveness wins.*

ISOBEL   I love you.

BEN   NO!!

ISOBEL   *You took my last breath!*

BEN   Christ, I'm sick; I'm so sick.

ISOBEL   I want back my life. Give me back my life!

> *Players enter singing a religious-sounding chorale with a sense of sadness and triumph. They place a veil on* ISOBEL's *head. The actor playing* BEN *joins them.*

ISOBEL   *(an adult now)* I want to tell you now a secret. I was dead, was killed by Lion in long silver car. Starving Lion maul maul maul me to dead, with killing claws over and over my little young face and chest, over my chest my blood running out; he take my heart with. He take my heart with, in his pocket deep, but my heart talk. Talk and talk and never be quiet never be quiet. I came back.

I take my life. I want you all to take your life. I want you all to have your life.

Players sing a second, joyful chorale, walking off. ISOBEL *ascends, in her mind, into heaven. The last thing we see is her veil.*

The End

Acknowledgements

I would like to thank Gregor; Michael Ondaatje; Urjo Kareda; Bob Wallace; all the actors in the cast lists; both Sarahs; Jane Cairnie-Richardson; and Francesca, who held and rocked three-week-old Grace while I transformed the hour-long radio play called *A Big White Light* into *Lion in the Streets*. And, of course, Isobel.

Judith Thompson is a playwright, director, screenwriter, actor, and teacher of theatre, and is a two-time winner of the Governor General's Literary Award for *White Biting Dog* and *The Other Side of the Dark*. She has been invested as an Officer in the Order of Canada, was awarded the prestigious Susan Smith Blackburn Prize for her play *Palace of the End* in 2008, and won the 2009 Amnesty International Freedom of Expression Award for the same play. Judith is a professor of drama at the University of Guelph and lives with her husband and five children in Toronto.